WELSH NAMES FOR YOUR CHILDREN
The Complete Guide

Third Edition

compiled by
Meic Stephens

D1630806

ST DAVID'S PRESS
Cardiff

Published in Wales by St David's Press, an imprint of

Ashley Drake Publishing Ltd
PO Box 733
Cardiff
CF14 7ZY
www.ashleydrake.com

First Published – 2000
Second Edition – 2003
Third Edition – 2009

ISBN
978 1 902719 23-8

British Library Cataloguing-in-Publication Data.
A CIP catalogue for this book is available from the British Library.

Introduction

This book is a collection of approximately 2,150 Welsh first names. It is intended primarily for parents, or prospective parents, who are seeking a name, or names, for their children. In such a serious, but pleasant task they may need some practical advice, and they will find it here, in a form easy to follow and understand.

The names are arranged according to the English alphabet. For each there is an indication of whether it is masculine (m) or feminine (f), or both (mf). There follows, in many instances, an explanation of the name's constituent parts or semantic root, which are usually from Welsh (e.g. Cadwallon: *cad*, a battle + *gwallon*, a ruler). English cognates or equivalents are given (e.g. John: Siôn; Mary: Mair). Many of the entries end with a brief word about illustrious bearers of the name and some associated place-names are noted. Variant spellings of a name are grouped together (e.g. Eurion m, Euriona f, Euriana f), and can be quickly found by means of cross-references.

The Welsh language is particularly rich in first or Christian names. Many date from as early as the fifth century when the Britons, as the early Welsh were known, lived not only in western Britain but also in what are today the north of England and the lowlands of Scotland. They are usually the names of Celtic saints, or holy men, who gave their names to so many of the churches, and thus to the parishes, villages and towns, of Wales (e.g. Llanbadarn, the church of Padarn), or of the warriors whose courage at the battle of Catraeth in about the year 600 is celebrated in Aneirin's poem, *Y Gododdin*. Others have survived from the ancient Triads which commemorate the heroes and heroines of the Isle of Britain from an even earlier age. Many, particularly those associated with Arthur, are from the early medieval period, and are to be found mostly in the prose masterpiece known as the Mabinogion or in the work of the poets who sang the praises of the native princes and gentry of Wales.

It is always a keen pleasure when a child discovers that he or she is named after a distinguished man or woman. We in Wales are especially fond of such names as Owain, Angharad, Rhodri and Siwan, and the names of legendary figures such as Mabon and Ceridwen, and this book will provide ample choice for parents who share this preference. Many of these names are already in common use in Wales, and some are quite fashionable, but there is no reason whatsoever why they should not be given a wider currency. They may have greater resonance for the Welsh than for others, for they are inextricably linked with our history and literature, but they are nevertheless fine names of which any child can be proud. Since my notes on many of the historical and legendary figures are necessarily brief, I recommend that the reader who requires further information about them should consult the works listed in the select bibliography at the end of this book.

Like English, Welsh creates personal names from a variety of sources. Many fine examples have been formed from the names of the rivers, hills, lakes, villages and regions of Wales, such as Teifi (a river), Berwyn (a range of hills), Tegid (a lake), Nefyn (a village) and Dyfed (an ancient province) – some of which, let us remember, were personal names in the first instance. This process has continued into our own day and new names are being coined all the time: no longer are the Welsh confined to names like John and Ann, as we were until quite recently. In an attempt to keep abreast of this modern trend, I have cast an eye daily over the births, marriages and deaths columns for some thirty years. I am grateful to the many people from all parts of Wales who have drawn my attention to the uncommon or rare names borne by their relatives and friends. I have tried to be as eclectic as possible, including names which, though they may not be among my own favourites, are known to have been given to children at one time or another. For example, I was particularly glad to find, a few years ago, in the registers for a parish in Radnorshire, what strikes me as the beautiful name Cymbriana – presumably from Cymru, the Welsh word for Wales, and on the model of Gloriana – and although, as far as I know, no child bears it nowadays, I have included it here. One of the consequences of this method is that my collection is one of the largest ever compiled for the general reader and perhaps the most comprehensive ever published. I hasten to add that if readers would like to draw my attention to any names which have escaped my net, I hope they will contact me.

I should like to offer a word of advice to parents who find themselves attracted to a name which is in some way out of the ordinary: it is that they should have confidence in their own taste and choose it – but not before making sure they know its provenance. After all, Afagddu ('utter darkness'), for example, would perhaps be a difficult name for a child to bear, while Efnisien was the name of a notorious villain and Cacamwri seems to have comical connotations which are best avoided. They are nevertheless included here, since I have found that there is no accounting for taste in this very personal, not to say subjective, business of choosing names for children, and the world is not yet so uniformly grey that there is no room left for rare, or uncommon, names. I am still rather fond of Cymbriana and hope one day to see it bestowed again on a child. I trust, too, that readers of this book will soon have their own favourites.

This is not a work of original scholarship, but I have tried, wherever possible in a field where so little information is available to the layman, to note the semantic root of many names, however conjectural it may be; in some instances the onomastic explanation (e.g *ôl*, a footprint + *gwen*, white » Olwen) has been accepted for want of any other. Furthermore, since all languages borrow from others, I have noted a number of names such as Anni, Pawl and Robat which, despite their Welsh spelling, barely conceal their origins in other languages. I have also included diminutive and hypocoristic or pet forms such as Bedo for Maredudd and Guto for Gruffudd.

In my notes on derivations I have relied to a large extent on the expertise of the late Professor T.J.Morgan (1907–86), who was kind enough to help my wife, Ruth Stephens, in the compilation of her book, *Welsh Names for Children* (1970), which in turn provided a basis for Heini Gruffudd's book of the same title (1980). Dr Morgan was Professor of Welsh at the University College, Swansea. His book, *Welsh Surnames* (1985), written in collaboration with his son, Dr Prys Morgan, is the authoritative work on its subject. It explains, among other things, how the patronymic system (e.g. Dafydd ap Gwilym) worked in Wales and throws a good deal of light on how certain English surnames have their origins in the Welsh language (e.g. *coch*, red > Gouge, Gough).

Parents seeking advice on how to go about naming a child according to the old patronymic system, which has been partly revived in recent times, should consult a solicitor or registrar of births if they wish to adopt it in law, but it is a simple process: Dewi, the son of a man whose first name is Llywelyn can be named Dewi ap Llywelyn, and Dewi's son Rhys will be Rhys ap Dewi, and so on. Alternatively, the surname can be dropped altogether. For example, a girl given the names Eleri Maelor by parents surnamed Jones, can be called Eleri Maelor if her parents so wish or, as an adult, can choose to use those names alone; the use of *ach* (the daughter of) has not been revived as strongly as *ap* or *ab* (the son of, the equivalent of *mac* in Irish and Gaelic). But the patronymic system, which is particularly fashionable in the world of Welsh television and theatre, together with the dropping of anglicized surnames, adds to the rich variety of how people are named in Wales and reflects, moreover, a growing pride in our national identity.

Finally, the curious reader may like to know the names of my own children and grandchildren. My wife and I have three daughters, Lowri Angharad, Heledd Melangell, and Brengain Gwenllian; a son, Huw Meredydd; and nine grandchildren, Elan Meredydd, Rhiannon Wyn, Gwern Arthur, Martha Glain, Gwenno Angharad, Begw Angharad, Elis Rhys, Luned Rhys, Gethin Emrys and Menna Llwyd. It is to the last of these, citizens of Wales in the twenty-first century, that I should like to dedicate this book.

Meic Stephens
Whitchurch, Cardiff
August 2009

Cyflwynir y llyfr hwn i

ELAN MEREDYDD
RHIANNON WYN
GWERN ARTHUR
MARTHA GLAIN
GWENNO ANGHARAD
BEGW ANGHARAD
ELIS RHYS
LUNED RHYS
GETHIN EMRYS
MENNA LLWYD

dinasyddion Cymru yn yr unfed ganrif ar hugain

A Note on the Pronunciation of Welsh

Welsh is not so difficult to pronounce as many people seem to assume on first encountering it. The language is largely phonetic, its sounds being, on the whole and compared with those of English, fairly consistent, so that once the basic rules are mastered, pronunciation is relatively straightforward.

The consonants, of which there are twenty-one, usually have the same sounds as in English, but with the following exceptions: *c* is always pronounced as in cat, *ch* as in loch, *dd* as in thou, *f* as in of, *ff* as in off, *g* as in god, *ng* as in singing or finger, *h* as in house, *ll* as in antler, *r* as in horrid, *rh* as in rhododendron, *s* as in son, *si* as in shoe, and *th* as in think. Here are some names illustrating these rules: Catrin, Desach, Heledd, Ifor, Ffion, Glyn, Brengain, Hywel, Llio, Rolant, Rhys, Seren, Siôn, and Gwenith.

The seven vowels are *a, e, i, o, u, w* and *y*, all of which represent pure vowel-sounds and not diphthongs as in English. They can be long or short, and a circumflex accent is sometimes used to denote the former, as in the name Siân. As a general rule vowels are long when followed by *b, ch, d, dd, f, ff, g, s*, and *th*, and short when followed by more than one consonant or by *c, ng, m, p* and *t*. The vowel *a* is pronounced as in palm (when long) or in hat (when short); *e* (when long) is similar to the sound in the French word *très* or (when short) is pronounced as in pen; *i* can be vocalic and long as in feed, or short as in lip, or consonantal as in young; *o* is pronounced as in door (when long) or hot (when short); *u* is similar to long and short *i*, except in north-west Wales where it resembles the vowel in the French pronoun *tu; w* is pronounced as in school (when long) or in cook (when short), or when consonantal as in war; *y* in final syllables is like the long or short vocalic *i*, but in non-final syllables it is like the u in further (when long) or in gun (when short). There are no silent letters and j, k, q, v, x and z occur only in words borrowed from other languages and, in the case of k and v, in archaic orthography.

Welsh in its written form has sixteen diphthongs, in all of which the principal vowel comes first. In the Welsh of south Wales they fall into two groups. Those ending on a close front vowel are *ae, ai, au* as in aye aye; *ei, eu, ey* as in day; *oe, oi, ou* as in boy; and *wy* which has no English equivalent but is pronounced oo + ee; those ending on a back rounded vowel are *aw* as in miaow, *iw, uw, yw* as in yew, *ew* (the short *e* followed by oo), and *ow* as in cow. In the Welsh of north Wales the diphthongs are *ae, au, eu, ey, oe, ou*, and *wy*, all of which end on a close central vowel. The variations between pronunciation in north and south Wales have no effect on mutual understanding. The reader should also bear in mind that Welsh, although euphonious, has an essentially robust character and is not to be spoken mincingly or through pursed lips. The accent usually falls on the penultimate syllable: e.g. Dáfydd, Myfánwy.

Further details about the pronunciation of Welsh will be found in the introduction to Bruce Griffiths and Dafydd Glyn Jones, *The Welsh Academy English-Welsh Dictionary* (1995). Also set out there are the rules governing the soft, nasal and spirant mutation of initial consonants and the aspiration of vowels, a feature which Welsh has in common with other Celtic languages.

A

ABEROG (m)

ABLOEG (m) AFLOEG (m)

Havelock (of Viking origin).
Afloeg was one of the sons of Cunedda.

ADARYN (f)

see Aderyn and Ederyn.

ADDA (m)

from Hebrew, red or the colour of skin.
Adam.
According to the New Testament, Adam
was the first man created by God; Eve
was his wife. Adda Fras, a poet of the
13th century, was said to have been buried in the abbey of Maenan in the Conwy
valley. Adda is also the name of a river
near Bangor in Gwynedd.

ADDAF (m)

ADDAON (m)

The son of Taliesin, Addaon was named
in the Triads as 'the most eloquent and
wisest young man to be found in the Isle
of Britain'.

ADDONWY (m)

A warrior named in *Y Gododdin* who, at
the battle of Catraeth, 'gave no quarter
to the Saxons'.

ADDONNA (f)

ADEON (m)

ADERYN (f) ADARYN (f) EDERYN (m)

a bird.

ADLAIS (f)

an echo.

ADRINA (f)

ADWEN (f)

from *gwen*, white or blessèd.
An early British saint.

AEDD (m)

According to legend, Aedd Mawr was
the father of Prydain, the legendary
founder of the Isle of Britain; the Britons
or early Welsh sometimes called themselves 'the progeny of Aedd Mawr'.

AEDDAN (m)

In *Y Gododdin*, Aeddan was one of the
heroes who 'paid for their mead-feast
with their lives'.

AEDDON (m)

An Anglesey chieftain whose elegy
appears in *The Book of Taliesin*.

AELHAEARN (m) ELHAEARN (m)

ael, a brow + *haearn*, iron.
A 7th-century saint to whom churches
at Gwyddelwern in Meirionydd and
Llanaelhaearn in Gwynedd are consecrated; his feast-day is 1 November.

A

AELWEN (f)

see Aelwyn.

AELWYN (m) AELWEN (f) AYLWYN (m)

ael, a brow + *gwyn* or *gwen*, white.

AERAM (m)

AERES (f)

an heiress.

AERFEN (f)

from *aer*, a battle.
A river-goddess revered by the Celts
who is associated with the river Dee.

AERGOL (m)

Aergol Lawhir (the Generous) was king
of Dyfed in the 6th century and patron
of St. Teilo.

AERIONYDD (f)

AERON (mf) AERONA (f)
AERONWEN (f) AERONWY (f)

aer, a battle + suffix, *on*.
from the Celtic Agrona, a god of battle
The town of Aberaeron in Ceredigion
stands on the river Aeron.

AERONA (f)

see Aeron.

AERONWEN (f)

see Aeron.

AERONWY (f)

see Aeron.

AETHWY (m)

Porthaethwy is the Welsh name of the
village of Menai Bridge in Anglesey.

AFAGDDU (m)

utter darkness.
An alternative name for Morfran in the
Mabinogion.

AFALLACH (m)

According to the royal genealogies,
Afallach was the grandson of Beli
Mawr. Ynys Afallach was the name of
the ideal country to which King Arthur
was taken and which was later known
as Afallon (E. Avalon).

AFALLON (m)

from *afallen*, an apple-tree.
The place-name Avalon in Arthurian romance is derived from Afallon.

AFAN (m) AFEN (m)

A Celtic saint, the cousin of St. David, to
whom churches are consecrated at
Llanafan Fawr in Powys and Llanafan in
Ceredigion. Afan Ferddig was a poet in
the 7th century. The town of Aberafan
stands on the estuary of the river Afan.

AFANDROG (m)

AFAON (m)

He is named in the Triads as one of 'the
Three Bull Chieftains of the Isle of
Britain'.

AFARWY (m)

The son of Lludd, king of Britain, according to Geoffrey of Monmouth in his *History of the Kings of Britain* (c. 1136).

AFEN (m)

see Afan.

AFLOEG (m)

see Abloeg.

AFONWY (f)

AFRYL (f)

from Avril.

AIDAN (m)

A 6th-century saint, a pupil of St. David, whose feast-day is 31 January.

AITHWEN (f)

ALAFON (m)

The bardic name of Owen Griffith Owen (1847–1916)

ALAN (m) ALON (m)

An early Welsh saint who became bishop of Quimper in Brittany; Alan Llwyd is one of the best contemporary Welsh poets.

ALAW (mf)

a melody.
A river in Anglesey on the banks of which, as related in the Mabinogion, Branwen died; the village of Trealaw is in the Rhondda valley.

ALAWN (m)

An early poet, according to tradition, about whom nothing is known.

ALBAN (m)

The first British martyr, in the 3rd century, whose name is the Welsh for modern Scotland.

ALCWYN (m)

from Alcuin (Old English).

ALDEN (m)

ALDITH (m) ALDYTH (f)
ALDWYTH (m)

from Ealdgyth (Old English).

ALDRYD (m) ALDRYDD (m)

The 9th-century king of Ewias, a district in the Black Mountains of Monmouthshire and what is today western Herefordshire.

ALDRYDD (m)

see Aldryd

ALDWYN (m)

from Ealdwine (Old English).

ALDWYTH (m)

see Aldith.

A

ALDYTH (f)

see Aldith.

ALED (m) ALEID (m)

A river in Denbighshire. Tudur Aled was one of the greatest Welsh poets of the 15th century. Aled Jones is a popular singer of our own day and Aled Islwyn a well-known novelist.

ALEID (m)

see Aled.

ALFOR (m)

ALFYN (m)

ALIS (f) ALYS (f)

from Alice (of Old German origin).
Alys Rhonwen was the daughter of Hengist; according to early tradition, Vortigern, leader of the British in the mid-5th century, fell in love with her and, as his wife, she encouraged the spread of Saxon rule over southern Britain. The English are sometimes called 'the children of Alice' by the Welsh.

ALLTWEN (f)

A village near Pontardawe in the Swansea Valley.

ALON (m)

see Alan.

ALUN (m) ALYN (m) ALUNA (f)

ALUNDA (f)

A river in Flintshire. Alun Mabon is the hero of a famous poem by John Ceiriog Hughes (1832–87); the poet Alun Lewis (1915–44) was from Aberdare.

ALUNA (f)

see Alun.

ALUNDA (f)

See Alun.

ALWEN (f) ALWYN (m)

A river in Clwyd; Alwyn Rice-Davies was the Anglican Archbishop of Wales.

ALWENYN (f)

ALWYN

see Alwen.

ALYN (M)

see Alun.

ALYS (f)

see Alis.

AMAETHON (m)

a farmer.
One of the children of Dôn, the god of agriculture; Culhwch, in the Mabinogion, in order to win Olwen, has to enlist the god's help in order to provide food and drink for the marriage-feast.

AMANWY (m)

The bardic name of David Griffiths (1882–1953) from the Amman valley in Carmarthenshire.

AMIG (m)

A character in a medieval tale partly set in the court of Charlemagne, in which, with that of his friend Amlyn, Amig's honour is put to a series of tests; the tale is the subject of a verse-play by Saunders Lewis, *Amlyn ac Amig* (1940).

AMLODD (m)

According to legend, Amlodd was the grandfather of King Arthur.

AMLYN (m)

see Amig.

AMNON (m)

The bardic name of Rees Jones (1797–1844) of Talgarreg in Ceredigion.

AMRANWEN (f)

amrant, an eyelid + *gwen*, white.

AMWEL (m)

ANARAWD (m)

an, intensifying prefix + *arawd*, speech or *rhawd*, a host.
Anarawd ap Gruffudd was a leader of the Welsh in south-west Wales in the 12th century.

ANDRAS (m)

Llanandras is the Welsh name for Presteigne, a town in Powys; the name is also a sobriquet for the Devil.

ANDREAS (m) ANDRO (m)

from Greek, manly.
Andrew.
The first disciple of Jesus was called Andrew.

ANDRO (m)

see Andreas.

ANEIRA (f)

an, intensifying prefix + *eira*, snow.

ANEIRIN (m) ANEURIN (m) NEIRIN (m)

The poet who wrote the heroic poem, *Y Gododdin*, which celebrates the death in battle of some 300 British warriors at the battle of Catraeth (c. 600) at a site thought to be near Catterick in what is today Yorkshire; nothing is known about him. Aneurin Bevan (1897–1960) was Labour MP for Ebbw Vale and a prominent member of the British Left; his name was often abbreviated to Nye.

ANEIRWEN (f)

ANELLYDD (m)

ANEST (f) ANNEST (f)

The daughter of Gruffudd ap Cynan, king of Gwynedd in the 12th century.

A

ANEURIN (m)

see Aneirin.

ANGELL (mf)

A river in Gwynedd.

ANGHARAD (f) ANGHARED (f)

an, intensifying prefix + *car*, loved.
The mother of Giraldus Cambrensis (c. 1146–1223) and the wife of Gruffudd ap Cynan (c. 1050–1137). Angharad Mair is a television presenter and marathon runner and Angharad Rees is an actress. The name is sometimes anglicized as Ankret and Anchoret.

ANGHARED (f)

see Angharad.

ANGWEN (f) ANGWYN (m)

an, intensifying prefix + *gwen, gwyn*, white or blessèd.

ANGWYN (m)

see Angwen.

ANHUN (m)

from Latin, Antonius.
Anthony.

ANIAN (m)

Anian was Bishop of St. Asaph in the 13th century.

ANLAWDD (m)

Anlawdd Wledig was the father of Goleudydd and grandfather of Culhwch, in the Mabinogion.

ANNALYN (f)

ANNEST (f)

see Anest.

ANNI (f)

Annie.

ANNORA (f)

ANNWEN (f) ANWEN (f)

an, intensifying prefix + *gwen*, white or blessèd.

ANNWYL (f) ANWYL (f)

dear, belovèd.

ANONA (f)

see Nona.

ANTUR (m)

adventure.

ANWEN (f)

see Annwen.

ANWYL (f)

see Annwyl.

ARAN (mf)

A mountain in Meirionydd.

ARANLI (m)

ARANRHOD (f)

see Arianrhod.

ARANWEN (f)

see Arianwen.

ARANWY (f)

ARAWN (m)

In the Mabinogion Arawn is king of the Underworld.

ARBAN (m)

The name of a stream in Powys.

ARDDUN (f)

beautiful, sublime.

ARDDUR (m)

Trearddur is a village in Anglesey.

ARDUDFYL (f)

see Tudful.

ARDUDWEN (f)

ARDWYNA (f)

AREINA (f)

ARFON (m) ARFONA (f) ARFONIA (f)

ar, opposite + *Môn*, Anglesey.
A district of the old county of Caernarfonshire, now in Gwynedd.

ARFONA (f)

see Arfon.

ARFONIA (f)

see Arfon.

ARFRYN (m)

from *bryn*, a hill.

ARGOED (m)

from *coed*, trees.
'Argoed of the secret places' was part of Gaul in a famous poem by T. Gwynn Jones (1871–1949).

ARIAL (m)

vigour, strength, courage.

ARIANDER (m)

ARIANNELL (f)

An early saint.

ARIANRHOD (f) ARANRHOD (f)

arian, silver + *rhod*, a circle
Arianrhod, the daughter of Dôn, was the Celtic moon-goddess and the goddess of poetic inspiration. In the Mabinogion she is the mother of Lleu Llaw Gyffes. Caer Arianrhod is the Welsh name for the *aurora borealis*.

ARIANWEN (f) ARIANWYN (m)

arian, silver + *gwen, gwyn*, white or blessèd.
An early saint, the daughter of Brychan Brycheiniog.

ARIANWYN (m)

see Arianwen.

ARIEL (m)

ARIFOR (m)

ARLWYDD (m)

ARMAEL (m)

ARMON (m)

The village of St. Harmon (Llanarmon) is in Powys.

ARNALLT (m)

Arnold

AROFAN (m)

The household poet of Selyf ap Cynan Garwyn in the 7th century.

ARON (m)

The brother of Moses; also a Celtic saint.

**ARTHEN (m) ARTHIAN (m)
ARTHIEN (m)**

A river-god; the son of Brychan Brycheiniog in the 5th century; the king of Ceredigion in the 9th century.

**ARTHFAEL (m) ARTHFEL (m)
ARTHMAEL (m)**

arth, a bear + *mael*, a prince.

ARTHFEL (m)

see Arthfael.

ARTHGAL (m)

ARTHGEN (m)

arth, a bear + *gen*, born of.

ARTHIEN (m)

see Arthen.

ARTHMAEL (m)

see Arthfael.

ARTHOG (m)

A village in Meirionydd.

ARTHUR (m)

from *arth*, a bear
The king of the Britons in the 6th century and later a figure in European literature. Little is known about the native Welsh Arthur but he was transformed in French and English literature into a hero of romance.

ARTHWEL (m)

ARTHWYS (m)

ARTRO (m)

A river in Gwynedd.

ARWEL (m)

Arwel Hughes (1909–88) was a distinguished Welsh composer.

ARWEN (f)

see Arwyn.

ARWENNA (f)

see Arwyn.

ARWYN (m) ARWEN (f) ARWENNA (f)

ar, intensifying prefix + *gwyn, gwen*, white or fair.

ASAFF (m)

A saint who founded the see of St. Asaph in what later became Denbighshire.

AUR (f)

gold.

AURES (f)

AURDDOLEN (f)

aur, gold + *dolen*, a link.

AURFRYN (m)

aur, gold + *bryn*, a hill.

AURIOLA (f)

AURLYS (f)

AURONA (f)

AURYN (m)

from *aur*, gold.

AWEL (f) AWELA (f)

a breeze.

AWELA (f)

see Awel.

AWEN (f) AWENA (f) ARWENNA (f)

a muse, inspiration.

AWENA (f)

see Awen.

AWSTIN (m)

from Latin, venerable.
Augustus, Augustine.
Augustine was the first Bishop of Canterbury, who came to Britain in the 6th century.

AYLWYN (m)

see Aelwyn.

B

BAEDDAN (m)

The name of a stream on the border between Powys and Monmouthshire.

BAGLAN (m)

An early saint whose memory survives in the place-name Baglan, a district of Port Talbot; the traditional belief was that his teacher, Illtud, gave him a staff with a brass crook (*baglan*), from which he took his name.

BALDWYN (m)

from Baldwin (Old English).

BANWEN (f)

ban, a peak + *gwen*, white.
A village in the Neath valley.

BARACH (m)

A stream in Carmarthenshire.

BARLWYD (m)

a stream near Blaenau Ffestiniog.

BARRI (m)

from Ynys Barren or Barre, now Barry Island.

BARRWG (m) BARUC (m)

A saint who was buried on Ynys Barren (Barry Island).

BARTI (m)

Bartholomew.
Barti Ddu or Black Bart was the sobriquet of Bartholomew Roberts (1682?–1722), a famous pirate from Pembrokeshire.

BARUC (m)

see Barrwg.

BARWYN (m)

BECA (f)

see Rebeca.

BECHAN (f)

small.
a variant of Bethan.
One of the daughters of Brychan Brycheiniog.

BEDAWS (m)

from *bedw*, a birch-tree.

BEDO (mf) BEDYN (mf)

the pet forms of Maredudd
There were four medieval poets who bore this name: Bedo Brwynllys (fl. 1400), Bedo Phylip Bach (fl. 1480), Bedo Aeddren (fl. 1500) and Bedo Hafesb (fl. 1567–85). The surname Beddoe is derived from Bedo.

BEDWIN (m)

see Bedwyn.

BEDWYN (m) BEDWIN (m)

from *bedw*, a birch-tree.

BEDWYR (m)

Bedivere.
One of Arthur's knights; he it was who, after the king's death, hurled the sword Excalibur into the lake. Bedwyr Lewis Jones (1933–92) was Professor of Welsh at the University of Bangor.

BEDYN (mf)

see Bedo.

BEGGAN (f)

a pet form of Margaret.

BEGW (f)

a pet form of Margaret.
This name was popularized by Kate Roberts in her book *Te yn y Grug* (1959).

BEINON (m)

ab Einon, the son of Einon.
This name has been anglicized to Beynon.

BELI (m)

Belenos was the sun god worshipped by the Celts. Beli Mawr was king of the Britons in the time of Julius Caesar; he may have been a mythical figure but the early heraldry shows that eminent families in Wales claimed descent from him.

BEN (m)

from Latin, *benedictus* or Welsh, *bendigaid*, blessèd.

BENDIGEIDFRAN (m)

see Brân.

BENLLI (m)

Benlli Gawr was said to be a tyrannical ruler of Powys whose citadel was destroyed by fire from heaven as punishment for his oppression of Garmon.

BERDDIG (m)

The court-poet of Gruffudd ap Llywelyn who ruled Gwynedd in the 11th century.

BERE (m)

A castle built by the Welsh to guard the southern boundary of Gwynedd in the early 13th century.

BERGAM (m)

A poet whose manuscripts date from the 14th century.

BERIAN (m)

Brynberian is a village near Crymych, in north Pembrokeshire.

BERIS (f)

BERNANT (m)

BERROG (m)

BERTH (f)

BERTHEN (m)

BERW (m)

BERWEN (f)

see Berwyn.

BERWIN (m)

see Berwyn.

BERWYN (m) BERWIN (m) BERWEN (f)

bar, a mound or peak + *gwyn*, white.
An early Welsh saint who gave his name to a range of hills in what are today Meirionydd and Denbighshire. Berwyn Price won a gold medal for Wales in the 110 metre hurdles at the 1978 Commonwealth Games.

BESSI (f)

see Bet.

BET (f) BETI (f) BETHAN (f) BETSAN (f) BETSI (f) BESSI (f)

diminutive forms of Elisabeth.
Betty.

BETHAN (f)

see Bet.

BETI (f)

see Bet.

BETRYS (f)

Beatrice.

BETSAN (f)

see Bet.

BETSI (f)

see Bet.

BEUNO (m)

A 7th-century saint who became the patron saint of Gwynedd; his most important church is at Clynnog and his feast-day is 21 April.

BIFAN (m)

ab Ifan, the son of Ifan.
This name has been anglicized as Bevan.

BILO (m)

a pet form of Wiliam.

BLADUD (m)

The son of Rhun is said to have succeeded his father as king of north Britain. Geoffrey of Monmouth maintained that the city of Bath was built by his order and that he fell to his death while attempting to fly.

BLAEN (m)

A warrior who took part in the battle of Catraeth; he is praised in *Y Gododdin* because of his generosity in peace and courage in battle.

BLEDDYN (m) BLEIDDYN (m)

from *blaidd*, a wolf.
He accompanied Garmon to Wales in the 5th century. Bleddyn ap Cynfryn was an 11th-century prince. Bleddyn Williams and Bleddyn Bowen were distinguished international rugby players in the 1950s and 1980s respectively.

BLEDIG (m) BLEDUC (m)

A bishop of St. David's in the 10th century.

BLEDRI (m)

blaidd, a wolf + *rhi*, a ruler.
Bledri ap Cydifor (fl. early 13th century) was an interpreter who is believed to have introduced Welsh legends to the Normans and so into the literatures of Europe.

BLEDRWS (m)

Betws Bledrws is a hamlet in Ceredigion.

BLEDUC (m)

see Bledig.

BLEGORED (m)

see Blegywryd.

BLEGYWRYD (m) BLEGORED (m)

A scholar who took part in Hywel Dda's law councils in the 10th century.

BLEIDDAN (m) BLEIDDFAN (m)

from *blaidd*, a wolf.

BLEIDDFAN (m)

see Bleiddan.

BLEIDDIG (m)

from *blaidd*, a wolf.

BLEIDDUD (m)

blaidd, a wolf + *udd*, a ruler/
A bishop of St. David's in the 12th century

BLEIDDYN (m)

see Bleddyn.

BLETRWS (m)

BLODEUWEDD (f)

blodau, flowers + *gwedd*, countenance
The wife of Lleu Llaw Gyffes in the fourth branch of the Mabinogion, made by Math ap Mathonwy from flowers; when she proved unfaithful she was changed into an owl. The tale is the subject of a verse-play by Saunders Lewis (1893–1985).

BLODITH (F)

BLODWEN (f)

blodau, flowers + *gwen*, white or blessèd.

BLODYN (f)

a flower.

BLWCHFARDD (m)

A poet who lived in the north of Britain in the 6th century.

BOBI (m)

the diminutive form of Robert.
Bobi Jones is one of the most distinguished of contemporary Welsh writers.

BODFAN (f)

BODFEL (m)

BODGAD (m)

A warrior whose courage is celebrated in *Y Gododdin*.

BODYCHEN (m)

a mansion in Anglesey.

BONFYL (m)

BOREUGWYN (m)

bore, morning + *gwyn*, fair.

BOWEN (m)

ab Owen, the son of Owen. Cardiff-born Jeremy Bowen is a renowned television journalist and broadcaster.

BRADACH (m)

The name of a stream in Monmouthshire.

BRADWEN (m)

A man mentioned in the tale of Culhwch and Olwen.

BRAINT (mf)

honour, privilege.
The name is connected with Briganti (the exalted one), a Celtic goddess.

BRÂN (m)

a crow.
A form of Bendigeidfran, the son of Llŷr (Lear), and son of Beli according to tradition. In the second branch of the Mabinogion Brân is king of Britain and, of gigantic build, wades across the sea to avenge his sister Branwen in Ireland. He may have been a half-human form of one of the ancient Celtic gods.

BRANWALADR (m)

BRANWEN (f)

The wife of Matholwch, king of Ireland, and sister of Brân (Bendigeidfran), the heroine of the second branch of the Mabinogion. She is ill-treated in Ireland but sends a starling to inform her brother of her plight. Brân then invades Ireland, rescues Branwen and returns to Britain with seven survivors of the conflict. But Branwen, appalled that the two islands have been laid waste because of her, dies of a broken heart on the banks of the Alaw in Anglesey.

BREICHIAWL (m)

A warrior whose courage is celebrated in *Y Gododdin*.

BRENGAIN (f) BRENGWAIN (f) BRENGIEN (f)

The hand-maiden of Esyllt in the medieval tale of Trystan and Esyllt (Iseult); it is she who gives them the fateful love-potion. She appears as Brengana in Wagner's opera *Tristan und Isolde*.

BRENGIEN (f)

see Brengain.

BRENGWAIN (f)

see Brengain.

BRENNIG (f)

A stream and lake in Dyfed, and a stream in north-east Wales with its source in Llyn Brân.

BREUAN (m)

Brian, Bryan.

BRIAFAEL (m)

from *bri*, fame, distinction
An early saint.

BRIALLEN (f)

a primrose.

BRIALLT (f)

BRIANNE (f)

Llyn Brianne is a reservoir in Carmarthenshire.

BRILLWEN (f)

see Ebrillwen.

BRINLI (m) BRYNLE (m)

Brinley.

BRIOC (m)

A 6th-century saint, with a church at Llandyfriog in Ceredigion, who is also remembered in place-names in Cornwall and Brittany.

BRIOG (m) TYFYRIOG (m)

Briog is a pet form of Briafael.
A 5th-century saint from Ceredigion who was educated by Bishop Garmon in Paris.

BRIWNANT (m)

BROCHAN (m)

from Brychan
A stream to the north of Llangurig in Powys.

BROCHFAEL (m) BROCHWEL (m)

Brochfael Ysgythrog was prince of Powys in the 6th century; it was against his hounds that Melangell is said to have shielded the hare.

BROCHWEL (m)

see Brochfael.

BRONGWYN (m)

see Bronwen.

BRONMAI (f)

bron, a hill or breast + *Mai*, May.

BRONWEN (f) BRONGWYN (m)

bron, a breast + *gwen* and *gwyn*, white.

BROTHEN (m)

An early saint who is commemorated at Llanfrothen in Meirionydd.

BRWYNO (m)

brwyn, sad or perhaps reeds.
There is a small valley known as Cwm Brwyno in Ceredigion.

BRWYNOG (m)

BRYAN (m) BRYANA (f) BRYNA (f)

Bryan.

BRYANA (f)

see Bryan.

BRYCHAN (m)

A 5th-century prince who gave his name to Brycheiniog, later known as Breconshire. According to tradition he had numerous children, many of whom became saints; his feast-day is 6 April.

BRYFDIR (m)

BRYN (m)

a hill.

BRYNA (f)

see Bryan.

BRYNCIR (m)

A village in Gwynedd.

BRYNACH (m) BYRNACH (m)

An early saint who came to west Wales from Ireland; his feast-day is 7 April.

BRYNEILEN (m)

BRYNGWYN (m)

bryn, a hill + *gwyn*, white.

BRYNIOG (m)

hilly.

BRYNLE (m)

see Brinli.

BRYNLLYN (m)

see Brynlyn.

BRYNLYN (m) BRYNLLYN (m)

BRYNMOR (m)

bryn, a hill + *mor*, large.
Brynmor Williams played rugby for Wales and the British Lions in the 1980s.

BRYNNER (m)

BRYTHON (m) BRYTHONEG (f)

Briton and British.

BRYTHONEG (f)

see Brython.

BRYTHONWEN (f)

Briton + *gwen*, white or blessèd.

BUDDFAEL (m)

BUDDFAN (m)

A warrior whose courage is celebrated in *Y Gododdin*, of whom it is said, 'The poets of the world judged him to be a man of courage'.

BUDDUG (f)

The queen of the Iceni, a British tribe who fought the Romans in the 1st century AD; she is reputed to have taken poison rather than fall into the invaders' hands. She is also known as Boadicea, Boudicca and Victoria.

BURWYN (m)

BYRNACH (m)

see Brynach.

C

CACAMWRI (m)

A comical character in the tale of Culhwch and Olwen; he shows such enthusiasm while threshing in a barn with an iron flail that he reduces the rafters to splinters.

CADAN (m)

from *cad*, a battle.
A stream in Dyfed.

CADEL (m)

see Cadell.

CADELL (m) CADEL (m)

Cadell ap Gruffudd was leader of the Welsh against the Normans in south Wales during the 12th century.

CADEYRN (m)

cad, a battle + *teyrn*, a ruler.

CADFAEL (m) CADMAEL (m) CATHMAEL (m)

cad, a battle + *mael*, a prince.
An early saint. Brother Cadfael is the monk who turns detective in a series of novels by Ellis Peters, the pseudonym of Edith Pargeter (1913–95).

CADFAN (m) CADFANNAN (m)

cad, a battle + *ban*, a summit.
A 6th-century saint who founded a monastery on Bardsey in the 6th century; his feast-day is 1 November. The village of Llangadfan is in Powys.

CADFANNAN (m)

see Cadfan.

CADFARCH (m)

cad, a battle + *march*, a horse.

CADFRAWD (m)

cad, a battle + *brawd*, a brother.

CADHAEARN (m)

cad, a battle + *haearn*, iron.

CADI (f) CATI (f) CATWS (f)

The diminutive forms of Catrin.
Cadi Haf was the traditional character who took part in the festivities of May Day in north-east Wales. Twm Shon Cati, known as 'the Welsh Robin Hood', is the hero of a popular tale by T.J.Ll. Prichard (1790–1862).

CADIFOR (m) CEDIFOR (m) CYDIFOR (m)

Cadifor ap Collwyn was abbot of Llancarfan in the 9th century.

CADLEW (m)

see Cadlyw.

CADLYW (m) CADLEW (m)

cad, a battle + *llyw*, a chief.
With Aneirin, Cadraith and Cynon, Cadlew was one of the four survivors of the battle of Catraeth.

C

CADMAEL (m)

see Cadfael.

CADMAR (m)

see Cadmawr.

CADMAWR (m) CADMAR (m)

cad, a battle + *mawr*, great.

CADO (m) CADOC (m) CATWG (m)

forms of Cadfael.

CADOC (m)

see Cado.

CADOG (m)

A 5th-century saint who was one of the foremost religious leaders of his time; he is commemorated at churches in Llangadog in Carmarthenshire and Llangattock in Powys; the monastery he founded at Llancarfan in the Vale of Glamorgan was a famous centre of learning.

CADOR (m)

The earl of Cornwall in the tales of Arthur.

CADRAITH (m)

With Aneirin, Cadlew and Cynon, he was one of the four survivors of the battle of Catraeth.

CADRAWD (m) CADROD (m)

cad, a battle + *rhawd*, a host.

CADROD (m)

see Cadrawd.

CADWAL (m)

cad, a battle + *wal*, a wall or defence.

CADWALADR (m)

cad, a battle + *gwaladr*, a ruler
An early saint. Cadwaladr Fendigaid (the Blessèd) was prince of Gwynedd in the 7th century.

CADWALLON (m)

cad, a battle + *gwallon*, a ruler.
Cadwallon ap Cadfan was king of Gwynedd in the 7th century and became the only British ruler to overthrow an English dynasty when he defeated Edwin of Northumbria at the battle of Haethfelth (known in Welsh tradition as Meigen), thought to be Hatfield Chase in modern Yorkshire.

CADWEL (m)

CADWGAN (m)

Cadwgan ab Owain was lord of south Wales in the 9th century. Moel Cadwgan is a mountain above the Rhondda valley. The name has been anglicized as Cadogan.

CAEO (m)

see Caio.

CAERENIG (m)

18

C

CAERON (m)

a stream near Penygroes, Gwynedd

CAERWYN (m)

caer, a fort + *gwyn*, white
J.E. Caerwyn Williams (1912–99) was a
distinguished Welsh scholar.

CAFFO (m)

A disciple of St. Cybi in the 6th century,
after whom Llangaffo in Anglesey is
named

CAI (m) CAW (m)

from Latin, Caius
An officer in Arthur's court who, in the
Mabinogion, was reputed to have been
able to go without sleep or hold his breath
under water for nine days and nights

CAIN (f)

fair, beautiful
One of the daughters of Brychan; she is
commemorated at Llangain in
Carmarthenshire and her feast-day is 8
October. The name is not to be confused
with that of Abel's brother.

CAINWEN (f)

see Ceinwen

CAIO (m) CAEO (m)

A village in Carmarthenshire. Julian Cayo
Evans, the self-styled Commandant of
the Free Wales Army during the 1960s,
took his sobriquet from the village's
name.

CALAN (f)

New Year's Day.

CALEB (m)

CALEDFRYN (m)

caled, hard + *bryn*, a hill.
The bardic name of William Williams
(1801–69), poet and critic.

CALLWEN (m)

see Cellan.

CAMARCH (m)

A stream in Powys.

CAMBER (m)

One of the three sons of Brutus after
whom, according to Geoffrey of
Monmouth, Wales was called in Latin,
Cambria; there is no historical evidence
for this assertion. Arwel Camber Thomas
has played rugby for Wales.

CAMWY (m)

a river in Patagonia.

CANTHRIG (f)

Canthrig Bwt was reputed to be a giantess who ate children and lived under a
cromlech near Llanberis in Gwynedd.

CARADAWG (m)

see Caradog.

CARADOC (m)

see Caradog.

C

CARADOG (m) CARADOC (m)
CRADOG (m) CARADAWG (m)

The leader of the Britons against the Roman invaders in the 1st century who, captured and taken in chains to Rome, was released on condition that he made no attempt to leave the city. He is also known by the Latin form of his name, Caratacus. The name has been anglicized as Craddock. Caradog Prichard (1904–80) was a distinguished Welsh novelist and poet.

CARANNOG (m) CRANNOG (m)

A 6th-century saint who is commemorated at Llangrannog in Ceredigion.

CAREDIG (m)

see Ceredig.

CAREN (f)

Karen.

CARI (f)

a diminutive form of Ceridwen.

CARIANWG (m)

CARINWEN (f)

CAROLWEN (f)

CARON (f)

A saint who is commemorated at Tregaron in Ceredigion.

CARONWYN (m)

caron + *gwyn*, white or blessèd.

CARREG (m)

a stone.

CARWEDD (m)

CARWEN (f) CARWYN (m)
CARWENNA (f)

câr, love + *gwen*, white or blessèd. Carwyn James (1929–83) was a renowned rugby coach. Carwyn Jones is a Labour member of the National Assembly.

CARWENNA (f)

see Carwen.

CARWYN (m)

see Carwen.

CARYL (f)

Carol.
Caryl Parry Jones is a popular entertainer on Welsh television.

CARYS (f)

CASNODYN (m)

A poet (fl. 1320–40) from Kilvey, now part of Swansea.

CASWALLON (m)

The son of Beli was leader of the Britons against the Roman invaders in the 1st century AD; it may be that the name retains a memory of Cassivellaunus, king of the Catuvellauni and leader of the Britons against Julius Caesar in 54 BC.

CATHAN (m)

20

CATHMAEL (m)

see Cadfael.

CATI (f)

see Cadi.

CATRIN (f)

from German, then Latin, pure.
Catrin of Berain (1534–91) was known as 'the Mother of Wales' on account of her four marriages and many children. The actress Catrin Fychan appeared in the Oscar-nominated film *Hedd Wyn* (1992).

CATWG (m)

see Cadog.

CATWS (f)

see Cadi.

CAW (m)

see Cai.

CAWRDAF (m)

from *cawr*, a giant.
The bardic name of William Ellis Jones (1795–1848).

CEDEWAIN (m)

The village of Betws Cedewain is in Powys.

CEDI (m)

A stream in Powys.

CEDIFOR (m)

see Cadifor.

CEDRYCH (m)

see Ceidrych.

CEDRYN (m)

CEDWYN (m)

An early saint who is commemorated at Llangedwyn in Clwyd.

CEFIN (m)

see Cefyn.

CEFNI (m)

A saint commemorated at Llangefni in Anglesey.

CEFYN (m) CEFIN (m)

Kevin.

CEIDIO (m) CEIDIOG (mf)

An early saint and a river in Gwynedd.

CEIDIOG (mf)

see Ceidio.

CEIDRYCH (m) KEIDRYCH (m)

perhaps a form of Caradog
A river in Carmarthenshire. The writer Keidrych Rhys (1915–87) adopted the name for literary purposes; Keidrych is the old spelling of the name.

CEINDEG (f)

cain, beautiful + *teg*, fair.

CEINDRYCH (f)

cain, beautiful + *drych*, appearance.

CEINFAN (f)

CEINFRYN (m)

cain, beautiful + *bryn*, a hill.

CEINLYS (f)

cain, beautiful + *melys*, fair.

CEINOR (f)

CEINWEN (f) CAINWEN (f)

cain, beautiful + *gwen*, white or blessèd
A saint, one of the daughters of Brychan,
who established a cell in Anglesey in the
5th century, where she is commemorated
at Llangeinwen.

CEIRI (m)

CEIRIAD (f)

from *caru*, to love.

CEIRIDWEN (f)

see Ceridwen.

CEIRIOG (m)

A river and valley in Clwyd from which
the poet John Ceiriog Hughes (1832–87)
took his bardic name.

CEIRION (f)

The Welsh name for Much Dewchurch in
Herefordshire is Llanddewi Rhos Ceirion.

CEIRIOS (f)

cherries.

CEIRO (m)

A stream in Ceredigion.

CEIRYNNEN (f)

CEIRYNWEN (f)

CEITHO (f)

An early saint who is commemorated at
Llangeitho in Ceredigion.

CELERT (m)

An early saint associated with
Beddgelert in Gwynedd. The tradition
that the village's name commemorates
Gelert, the dog of Llywelyn Fawr, is without foundation.

CELFRYN (m)

CELLAN (m) CALLWEN (m)

Cellan is a village in Ceredigion which
commemorates the saint Callwen.

CELT (m) KELT (m)

In the old orthography the name was written as Kelt.

CELYDDON (m)

The Welsh name for Caledonia (Scotland)

C

CELYN (mf)

holly.

CELYNEN (f) CELYNIN (f) CELYNOG (f)

One of the five saints commemorated at Llanpumsaint in Ceredigion.

CELYNIN (f)

see Celynen.

CELYNOG (f)

see Celynen.

CELYNYDD (m)

CEMLYN (m)

A village in Anglesey.

CENAU (m)

see Ceneu.

CENECH (m)

CENEU (m) CENAU (m)

offspring or a cub.

CENNARD (m)

from Irish, *ceann*, a head or *ceannacht*, a chieftain.

CENNIN (f)

CENNYDD (m) CENYDD (m)

A 6th-century saint, a son of Gildas, who is associated with Senghennydd and Llangennydd.

CENRED (m)

CENWYN (m)

cen, a head + *gwyn*, white or blessèd.

CENYDD (m)

see Cennydd.

CEREDIG (m) CAREDIG (m)

One of the sons of Cunedda, whose ancestors ruled Ceredigion for four centuries. Huw Ceredig is a well-known character actor on Welsh television.

CERI (mf)

A river in Dyfed and a village, Porth Ceri, near Barry in the Vale of Glamorgan. Ceri Richards (1903–71) was a disinguished Welsh painter.

CERIAN (f)

perhaps a combination of Ceri and Ann.

CERIDWEN (f) CEIRIDWEN (f)

The wife of Tegid Foel and mother of Taliesin; also the goddess of poetic inspiration. She brews a magic cauldron from which she intends her son Morfran (Afagddu) to drink and by so doing become imbued with the gift of poetry. Instead it is her servant, Gwion, who swallows a drop from the cauldron and, after many metamorphoses, he is renamed Taliesin.

23

C

CERIL (f) CERILYS (f)

CERILAN (f)

A combination of Ceridwen and Alan.

CERILYS (f)

see Ceril.

CERIS (f)

see Cerys.

CERIST (f)

A stream in Powys.

CERITH (m)

CERNYW (m)

The Welsh name for Cornwall. The village of Llangernyw is in Clwyd.

CERREN (f)

CERWYN (m)

CERYS (f) CERIS (f)

from *caru*, to love.
perhaps a diminutive form of Ceridwen
Cerys Matthews was lead-singer with the Welsh band Catatonia.

CEULAN (m) CEULANYDD (m)

The Ceulan is a stream in Ceredigion.

CEWYDD (m)

Cewydd ap Caw was a saint who was

associated with the belief that if it rained on his feast-day, 1 July, it would rain for forty days thereafter; his English equivalent is St. Swithin.

CIAN (m)

A poet renowned in the 5th century, about whom nothing is now known. Cian Clowes performs with the Super Furry Animals.

CIARAN (m)

CIBNO (m)

One of the warriors who were slain at the battle of Catraeth.

CIGFA (f)

The wife of Pryderi in the Mabinogion.

CILLYN (m)

CILMIN (m)

CILYDD (m)

A warrior, father of Tudfwlch, who took part in the battle of Catraeth.

CLAERWEN (f)

CLARIS (f)

Clarice, Clarissa.

CLEDAN (m)

The names of streams in Powys and Ceredigion.

CLEDDAU (mf)

a river in Pembrokeshire.

CLEDLYN (m)

caled, hard + *glyn*, a vale.
The Cledlyn is a stream in Ceredigion.

CLEDWYN (m)

caled, hard + *gwyn*, white or blessèd
A river in Denbighshire. Cledwyn Hughes
was Labour MP for Anglesey and the
second Secretary of State for Wales
(1966–68).

CLENNEL (m)

CLODDIEN (m)

CLODWYN (m)

CLWYD (mf)

An historic region and, from 1974–95, a
county in north-east Wales. Ann Clwyd
is Labour MP for the Cynon Valley.

CLYDAI (m)

A saint commemorated by a church near
Newcastle Emlyn in Carmarthenshire.

CLYDNO (m)

A prince of northern Britain who arrived
in Wales in the 6th century.

CLYDOG (m)

A saint and martyr who ruled Ewias, in
the Black Mountains and the western part
of Herefordshire, in the early 6th century.

CLYDRI (m)

A prince of Erging, the Welsh-speaking
part of what is today Herefordshire, in
the early 7th century.

CLYDWYN (m)

CLYNNOG (m)

A village in Gwynedd; Morys Clynnog
(1525–80) was a Catholic author.

COEL (m)

Coel Hen was reputed to have been the
progenitor of several royal dynasties,
including those of Urien Rheged and
Llywarch Hen; he is not to be confused
with 'Old King Cole', one of the ficti-
tious kings of Britain listed by Geoffrey
of Monmouth.

COETMOR (m)

COLLEN (m)

a hazel-tree.
A saint who established a cell at Llangollen
in the 6th century.

COLLFRYN (m)

COLLWEN (f)

An early saint.

C

COLLWYN (m)

Collwyn ap Tangno founded one of the royal families of Gwynedd in about 1020.

COLWYN (m)

A river in Conwy on which the town of Colwyn Bay stands.

CONWY (m)

A river on which the town of Conwy now stands.

CORRIS (m)

A village in Meirionydd.

CORWENNA (f)

CORWYN (m)

COTHI (mf)

A river in Ceredigion; Shân Cothi is a popular singer and broadcaster.

CRADOG (m)

see Caradog.

CRAIGFRYN (m)

craig, a rock + *bryn*, a hill.

CRALLO (m)

A saint to whom the church at Coychurch (Llangrallo), near Bridgend, is dedicated.

CRANNOG (m)

see Carannog.

CRANOGWEN (f)

The pseudonym of Sarah Jane Rees (1839–1916), writer and early feminist.

CREIDDYLAD (f)

see Creuddylad.

CREIRWY (f)

CREUDDYLAD (f) CREIDDYLAD (f)

Cordelia (Latin).

CREUNANT (m)

A village in the Dulais valley of Glamorgan; Alun Creunant Davies (1927–2005) was the first Director of the Welsh Books Council (1965–87).

CRINWEN (f)

CRISIANT (f)

crystal, bright.
The cousin of Owain Gwynedd (fl. 1150).

CRISTIOLUS (m)

A saint who is commemorated at Llangristiolus in Anglesey.

CRISTYN (f)

Cristina, Christine.

CRWYS (m)

a cross
The bardic name of William Williams (1875–1968), poet and preacher.

CUHELYN (m)

CULHWCH (m)

The hero of the tale of Culhwch and Olwen in the Mabinogion. In order to win her hand in marriage he has to accomplish a number of near-impossible tasks set by Olwen's father, the giant Ysbaddaden Pencawr, whom he eventually kills.

CUNEDDA (m)

The British leader who, in the 5th century, arrived in Wales from what is today Scotland with his eight sons, each of whom is reputed to have founded a royal dynasty.

CURIG (m)

A saint commemorated at Llangurig in Powys and Capel Curig in Gwynedd; his feast-day is 16 June.

CURWEN (m)

CWMWS (m)

CWELLYN (m)

The name of a lake in Gwynedd.

CWYFAN (m) CWYFEN (m)

An early saint who is commemorated at the church of Aberffraw in Anglesey.

CWYFEN (m)

see Cwyfan

CYBI (m)

A 6th-century saint who is commemorated

at Caergybi (Holyhead) in Anglesey; his feast-day is usually 5 (but also 6, 7 and 8) November.

CYCLYN (m)

CYDIFOR (m)

see Cadifor.

CYDWEL (m)

Cydweli is in Carmarthenshire.

CYDYWAL (m)

A warrior praised for prowess in battle at Catraeth where he was 'in the forefront of the men of Gwynedd'.

CYFEILIOG (m)

A district of Powys. Iorwerth Cyfeiliog Peate (1901–82) was a writer and first curator of the Welsh Folk Museum at St. Fagans, near Cardiff.

CYFFIN (m) KYFFIN (m)

The name of streams in Gwynedd and Ceredigion. Kyffin Williams (1918–2006) was a well-known painter of Welsh landscapes.

CYFWLCH (m)

One of Arthur's courtiers in the tale of Culhwch and Olwen.

CYLLIN (m)

CYMARON (m)

A stream in Powys.

C

CYMBRIANA (f)

from *Cymru*, Wales, presumably on the model of Gloriana, the name given to Elizabeth I in Spenser's *Faerie Queene* (1590–96).

CYMIDEI (f)

A giantess in the Mabinogion.

CYMON (m)

see Cynon.

CYMRAES (f)

a Welsh woman.

CYMRO (m)

a Welshman.

CYNAN (m)

The bardic name of poet and archdruid Albert Evans-Jones (1900–70).

CYNDDELW (m)

The greatest court-poet of the 12th century was Cynddelw Brydydd Mawr.

CYNDDYLAN (m)

Cynddylan ap Cyndrwyn was prince of Powys in the 7th century. His death and the fall of his household is lamented in saga verse by his sister Heledd.

CYNDDYLIG (m)

A character in the tale of Culhwch and Olwen and one of the sons of Llywarch Hen; the name also occurs as the title

of a long poem by T. Gwynn Jones (1871–1949).

CYNDEYRN (m)

cyn, chief + *teyrn*, lord.
A 6th-century saint commemorated at Llangyndeyrn in Carmarthenshire.

CYNDRIG (m)

see Cynfrig.

CYNFAB (m)

cyn, chief + *mab*, a son.

CYNFAEL (m) CYNFAL (m)

cyn, chief + *mael*, a prince.
A river in Gwynedd.

CYNFAEN (m) CYNFAN (m)

cyn, chief + *maen*, a stone.

CYNFAL (m)

see Cynfael.

CYNFAN (m)

see Cynfaen.

CYNFARCH (m) CYNMARCH (m)

cyn, chief + *march*, a horse.
A saint commemorated at Llanfair in Denbighshire.

CYNFELYN (m)

The father of Caradog; the name may be derived from Cunobelinus (Latin), Shakespeare's Cymbeline. Llangynfelyn is in Ceredigion.

CYNFERTH (m)

cyn, chief + *berth*, beautiful.

CYNFFIG (m) KYNFFIG (m)

A river near Margam on which Aberkenfig stands, near Bridgend.

CYNFOEL (m)

CYNFOR (m)

cyn, chief + *mawr*, great.
A pupil of St. Teilo.

CYNFRAN (m)

cyn, chief + *brân*, a crow.

CYNFRIG (m) CYNWRIG (m)
CYNRIG (m) CYNDRIG (m) KYNRIC (m)

Cynfrig ap Dafydd Goch was a poet in the mid-15th century.

CYNFYN (m)

Ysbyty Cynfyn is a village in Ceredigion.

CYNGAR (m)

A 6th-century saint who lived in Glamorgan and whose feast day is 7 or 27 November; the church at Llangefni in Anglesey is dedicated to him.

CYNGEN (m)

A prince who defended Powys against Saxon invaders in the 9th century.

CYNHAEARN (m)

cyn, chief + *haearn*, iron.

CYNHAFAL (m)

cyn, *chief* + *hafal*, equal
A saint in the 6th/7th century who is commemorated at Llangynhafal in Denbighshire.

CYNI (m)

see Cynri.

CYNIDR (m)

A 6th-century saint, a grandson of Brychan, who is commemorated at Llangynidr in Powys; his feast-day is 8 December.

CYNIN (m)

A saint commemorated at Llangynin in Gwynedd.

CYNLAIS (m)

A river on which Ystradgynlais in Powys now stands.

CYNLAS (m)

King of Britain in the 6th century who was attacked by Gildas.

CYNLLAITH (m)

CYNLLO (m)

A saint who is commemorated at Llangynllo in Powys; his feast-day is 17 July.

CYNMARCH (m)

see Cynfarch.

CYNNWR (m)

A saint who is commemorated at Llangynnwr in Carmarthenshire.

C

CYNOG (m)

A 6th-century saint, one of the sons of Brychan. Cynog Dafis is a senior Plaid Cymru leader and a founder member of the Welsh Language Society.

CYNOGAN (m)

A stream in north-east Wales.

CYNOLWYN (m)

The village of Abergynolwyn is in Meirionydd.

CYNON (m) CYMON (m)

A river flowing into the Taff at Abercynon; also a king of Gwynedd in the 9th century.

CYNRAIN (m)

A warrior whose prowess in battle is praised in *Y Gododdin*.

CYNRI (m) CYNI (m)

One of the warriors commemorated in *Y Gododdin*.

CYNRIG (m)

see Cynfrig.

CYNWAL (m)

cyn, chief + *gwal*, a wall or defence
One of the warriors whose courage is praised in *Y Gododdin*.

CYNWALLON (m)

CYNWIL (m)

see Cynwyl.

CYNWRIG (m)

see Cynfrig.

CYNWY (m)

CYNWYD (m)

An early saint who is commemorated at Llangynwyd in Bridgend.

CYNWYL (m) CYNWIL (m)

An early saint; also one of the three warriors who survived the battle of Camlann, according to the tale of Culhwch and Olwen.

CYNYR (m)

The father of Non and grandfather of Dewi Sant (St. David).

CYNYW (m)

A saint who is commemorated at Llangynyw in Powys.

CYSTENNIN (m)

from Latin, Constantius
One of the sons of Macsen Wledig.

CYWARCH (m)

A river near Dinas Mawddwy in Meirionydd.

CYWRYD (m)

An early saint.

D

DAFI (m)
Davy.
a pet form of Dafydd and David.

DAFINA (f)

DAFYDD (m)

from Hebrew, a loved one, a friend.
David.
Dafydd ap Gwilym (fl. 1315–70) was the
greatest Welsh poet of the medieval period. Dafydd Wigley is a senior figure
within Plaid Cymru.

DAI (m) DEI (m) DEIAN (m) DEIO (m)
DEICWS (m) DEICYN (m)

pet forms of Dafydd and David.

DALIS (m)

DALONI (f)

DALWYN (m)

tâl, a forehead + *gwyn*, white.

DARENWEN (f)

DARON (f)

dâr, an oak + suffix, *on*.
The goddess of the oak; also the name
of a river in Gwynedd on the estuary of
which the town of Aberdaron stands.

DARREN (m)

from *tarren*, burnt land or hill.

DARWEL (m)

DATHYL (f)

A woman mentioned in the Mabinogion.

DAVID (m)

see Dafydd.

DEDWYDD (mf)

happy.

DEFYNNOG (m)

see Dyfynnog.

DEGANWY (m)

The traditional site of the court of
Maelgwn Gwynedd; also a town on the
coast of north Wales.

DEGWEL (m)

see Dogfael.

DEI (m)

see Dai.

DEIAN (m)

see Dai.

D

DEICWS (m)

see Dai.

DEICYN (m)

see Deio.

DEILWEN (f)

deilen, a leaf + *gwen*, white.

DEINIOL (m)

A saint who established a church at Bangor in the 6th century.

DEION (m)

DEL (f)

pretty.

DELANA (f)

DELFRYN (m)

del, pretty + *bryn*, a hill.

DELOR (m)

see Telor.

DELUN (f)

del, pretty + *un*, one.

DELWEN (f) DELWYN (m)

del, pretty + *gwen, gwyn*, white.

DELWYN (m)

see Delwen.

DELYTH (f)

from *del*, pretty.

DELYN (f)

from *telyn*, a harp
Delyn is an electoral district in north-east Wales.

DENGAR (f)

DEOLYN (m)

DEREC (m)

Derek.
Derec Llwyd Morgan is a distinguished Welsh scholar and poet.

DERFAEL (m)

derw, an oak + *mael*, a prince.

DERFEL (m) DERFELA (f)

from *derw*, steadfast + *mael*, a prince
Derfel Gadarn was a saint who is commemorated at Llandderfel in Meirionnydd.

DERFELA (f)

see Derfel.

DERI (m)

oaks.

DERIS (f)

DERITH (f)

DERW (m)

see Derwen.

DERWEN (m) DERWENNA (f)
DERW (m)

an oak.

DERWYDD (m)

a druid.

DERWYN (m)

Derwyn Jones played rugby for Wales in the 1990s.

DERYN (f)

from *aderyn*, a bird.

DESACH (m)

A river in Gwynedd.

DEUANNA (f)

DEUDRAETH (m)

Penrhyndeudraeth is in Gwynedd.

DEULWYN (m)

perhaps from *dau*, two + *llwyn*, a grove.

DEWI (m)

Dewi Sant (fl. 6th century) is the patron saint of Wales; his feast-day is celebrated on 1 March. St. David's cathedral in Pembrokeshire is known in Welsh as Tŷ Ddewi.

DEWINA (f)

dewin, a wizard.

DIC (m)

Dick, the diminutive form of Richard
Dic Aberdaron (Richard Robert Jones, 1780–1843) was a well-known eccentric and Dic Penderyn (Richard Lewis, 1808–31) was executed for his alleged part in the Merthyr Rising of 1831. Dic Jones is one of the best contemporary poets writing in the traditional metres.

DIDDANWY (f)

see Dyddanwy.

DILWEN (f) DILWYN (m)

dil, a honeycomb + *gwen* or *gwyn*, white.

DILWYN (m)

see Dilwen.

DILYS (f)

genuine.
A name invented in the 19th century.

DINMAEL (m)

din, a fort + *mael*, prince.

DINOGAD (m)

A boy mentioned in an anonymous early poem, '*Pais Dinogad*'.

DION (m)

Many saints bore this name.

D

DIWRNACH (m)

Diwrnach Wyddel (the Irishman), in the tale of Culhwch and Olwen, is the owner of a cauldron which the hero has to procure as one of the conditions of winning Olwen's hand in marriage.

DOCHAU (m)

A saint who is commemorated at Llandochau (Llandough) near Cardiff.

DOERAN (m)

DOGFAEL (f) DOGMAEL (m)

A 6th-century saint, whose church is at St. Dogmael's (Llandudoch) in Pembrokeshire.

DOGMAEL (m)

see Dogfael.

DOIRAN (m)

DOLAN (m)

DÔN (f) DÔNA (f)

A Celtic goddess, also known as Danu; she is commemorated in the name of the river Donau (Danube).

DÔNA (f)

see Dôn.

DONWENNA (f)

DORIEL (f)

DORIEN (m)

DORTI (f)

a diminutive form of Dorothy.

DORWENA (f)

DOTWEN (f)

DROFANA (f)

DRUDWAS (m)

A character in the Mabinogion who owns a pair of fabulous birds.

DRUDWEN (f) DRYDWEN (f)

a starling.

DRYDWEN (f)

see Drudwen.

DRYSTAN (m)

see Trystan.

DULAIS (m) DULAS (m)

du, black + *clais*, a stream. Pontarddulais is a village in Carmarthenshire.

DULAS (m)

see Dulais.

DULI (m)

DULYN (mf)

The Welsh name for Dublin; there is a Cwm Dulyn near Penygroes in Gwynedd.

DUNAWD (m) DUNOD (m)

A 6th-century saint who is commemorated at St. Donats (Sain Dunawd) in the Vale of Glamorgan; his feast-day is 7 September.

DUNOD (m)

see Dunawd.

DWYFAN (f)

from the name of the river Dwyfor.

DWYFOR (f)

The name of a river which flows through Llanystumdwy in Gwynedd. David Lloyd George (1863–1945) took the name Earl Lloyd-George of Dwyfor.

DWYNWEN (f)

One of the daughters of Brychan and the patron saint of lovers, whose feast-day is celebrated on 25 January; she is the Welsh equivalent of St. Valentine (Ffolant).

DWYRYD (mf)

The name of a river in Gwynedd.

DWYSAN (f)

from *dwys*, profound.

DWYSLI (f)

DYBION (m)

The eldest son of Cunedda.

DYDDANWY (f) DIDDANWY (m)

from *diddanwch*, delight.

DYDDGEN (m)

DYDDGU (f)

The name of a dark-haired woman courted by the poet Dafydd ap Gwilym in the 14th century; she was the daughter of Ieuan ap Gruffudd ap Llywelyn whose home was at Tywyn in south Ceredigion. A contrast in every way to Morfudd, she was aristocratic, remote and virginal, remaining the unattainable object of the poet's affections.

DYFAN (m)

A missionary sent by the Pope to Britain in the 2nd century; he is commemorated at Merthyr Dyfan, near Barry. Dyfan Roberts is a popular actor.

DYFED (m) DYFEDWY (m)

One of the ancient regions of Wales, which includes the modern country of Pembrokeshire.

DYFEDWY (f)

see Dyfed.

DYFI (mf)

from *dyf*, dark or black.
A river in Gwynedd on the estuary of which the town of Aberdyfi stands.

DYFNALLT (m)

dwfn, deep + *allt*, a hill.
The bardic name of John Owen (1873–1956), archdruid.

DYFNWAL (m)

dyfn, deep + *gwal*, a defence.
Dyfnwal Moelmud is said to have ruled Wales in the 3rd century; the name has been anglicized as Devonald.

DYFNWALLON (m)

dyfn, deep + *gwallon*, a ruler.
Lord of Ceredigion in the 9th century.

DYFR (f)

She is named in the Triads as one of 'the Three Splendid Maidens of Arthur's court'.

DYFRI (m)

perhaps from *dwr*, water.
The name of a river that runs through Llanymddyfri (Llandovery) in Carmarthenshire.

DYFRIG (m)

An early saint whose feast-day is 14 November.

DYFYNNOG (m) DEFYNNOG (m)

A parish and village in Powys.

DYFYR (f) DYFIR (f)

A woman named in the Triads as one of 'the Three Splendid Maidens of Arthur's court'.

DYLAN (m)

The son of Arianrhod in the Mabinogion; at his birth he immediately took to the sea and was given the name Dylan Eil Ton (son of the wave). The name was unknown in modern Wales before it was given to the poet Dylan Thomas (1914–53).It is now quite popular: Woody Allen's daughter bears the name, as does the son of Catherine Zeta Jones.

DYNWAL (m)

DYNYS (m)

DYRFAL (m)

DYRINOS (m)

DYRNWCH (m)

E

EBEN (m)

from Hebrew, stone of help.
Eben Fardd was the bardic name of
Ebenezer Thomas (1802–63).

EBRILL (f) EBRILLA (f)

April.

EBRILLA (f)

see Ebrill.

EBRILLWEN (f) BRILLWEN (f)

Ebrill, April + *gwen*, white.

EDANA (f)

EDAR (m)

A warrior whose heroic death is described in *Y Gododdin*.

EDEILA (f)

EDERN (m)

The son of Nudd is a character in the
romance of Geraint fab Erbin. The village of Bodedern is in Anglesey.

EDERNOL (m)

from Latin, *eternalis*, eternal.

EDERYN (m)

see Aderyn.

EDFFRWD (m)

EDMWND (m) EMWNT (m)

Edmund.

EDNANT (m)

EDNO (m)

The name of a valley in Gwynedd.

EDNOWAIN (f)

EDNOWEN (m)

EDNYFED (m)

An early saint. Ednyfed Fychan was sen-
eschal of Gwynedd in the 13th century.

EDONA (f)

EDRYD (m)

EDWAL (m)

EDWART (m)

Edward.

EDWY (mf)

Aberedwy is a village in the Wye valley
in Powys.

E

EDWYN (m)

Edwin (Old English).

EDYS (f)

EFA (f)

Eva (Hebrew), Eve.

EFANNA (f)

EFLYN (f)

Evelyn.

EFNISIEN (m)

The cruel brother of Nisien in the Mabinogion; it is he who insults the Irish, the guests of Brân, by disfiguring their horses, thus causing conflict between Ireland and Britain.

EFNYDD (f)

EFROG (m)

The Welsh name for York; New York in Welsh is Efrog Newydd.

EFYR (m)

EGRYN (m)

A saint commemorated at Llanegryn in Meirionydd.

EGWAD (m)

EIC (m)

the pet form of Isaac.

EIDDEF (m)

A warrior praised in *Y Gododdin* for his speed and beauty.

EIDDIG (m)

from *aidd*, heat or ardour.

EIDDON (m)

EIDDWEN (f)

eiddun, fond or *aidd*, ardour + *gwen*, white.

EIDDYN (m)

see Eidin.

EIDIN (m) EIDDYN (m)

In *Y Gododdin* Caereidyn denotes the settlement which later became Edinburgh.

EIFION (m) EIFIONA (f)

One of Cunedda's sons. Eifion Wyn was the bardic name of Eliseus Williams (1867–1926).

EIFIONA (f)

see Eifion.

EIFLYN (f)

EIGON (m)

A saint who is commemorated at Llani-gon in Powys.

EIGR (f) EIGRA (f)

The wife of Gorlois, king of Cornwall, and mother of Arthur, was reputed to be the most beautiful woman in the Isle of Britain.

EIGRA (f)

see Eigr.

EILIAN (mf)

A saint commemorated at Llaneilian in Anglesey.

EILIONA (f)

EILIR (mf)

a butterfly.

EILIUDD (m)

An early saint.

EILRAD (f)

EILUNED (f)

see Eluned.

EILWEN (f) EILWYN (m)

eil, second + *gwen* and *gwyn*, white.

EILWYN (m)

see Eilwen.

EILYR (m)

EINION (m) EINIONA (f) ENIAWN (f)

an anvil.
Einion Yrth was one of Cunedda's sons.
Einion Offeiriad (fl.1320) wrote the first Welsh Grammar.

EINIONA (f)

see Einion.

EINIR (mf)

from Latin, *honora*, reputation.

EINON (m)

a variant of Einion.

EIOLYS (f)

EIRA (f)

snow.

EIRAL (f)

EIRAWEN (f) EIRWEN (f) EIRWYN (m)

eira, snow + *gwen, gwyn*, white.

EIRIAN (mf) EIRIANEDD (f) EIRIANELL (f) EIRIANA (f)

splendid, bright.
J. Eirian Davies (1918–98) was a well-known poet.

EIRIANA (f)

see Eirian.

EIRIANEDD (mf)

see Eirian.

EIRIANELL (f)

see Eirian.

E

EIRIG (m) EURIG (m)

fine or warlike.

EIRINWEN (f)

EIRIOES (f)

EIRIOL (f) EIRLYS (f)

a snowdrop.

EIRIOS (m)

bright or flame-coloured.

EIRYTH (f)

EIRLYS (f)

see Eiriol.

EIROS (m)

EIRWEL (m)

EIRWEN (f)

see Eirawen.

EIRWYN (m)

see Eirawen.

EIRY (f)

snow

EIRYL (f) EIRIL (m)

EIRYS (f)

an iris.

EIRYTH (f)

EITHINYN (m)

A warrior described in *Y Gododdin* as a magnificent horseman.

EITHRAS (f)

EITHWEN (f)

ELAETH (m)

A king who, after defeat by the Saxons in the 6th century, joined Siriol's monastery in Anglesey.

ELAI (m)

The Welsh name for the river Ely and district in Cardiff.

ELAIN (f)

a fawn.

ELAN (f) ELANNA (f)

The name of four streams in Ceredigion and Powys and of a mountain near Bethesda in Gwynedd. Elan Closs Stephens is a distinguished academic.

ELANNA (f)

see Elan.

ELANWEN (f) ELANWY (f)

ELDEG (m)

ELDRYD (m)

see Eldrydd.

ELDRYDD (mf) ELDRYD (m)

The Welsh versions of the name of a 10th-century king of the Saxons.

ELEN (f) ELIN (f) ELINA (f) ELENA (f) ELINNA (f)

from Greek, the bright one.
Helen
The woman known in Welsh tradition as Elen Luyddog (Helen of the Hosts) was the wife of Macsen Wledig, who became emperor of Rome. Elena Puw Morgan (1900–73) was a well-known Welsh novelist.

ELENA (f)

see Elen.

ELENID (f) ELENYDD (f)

A hilly district of Ceredigion where the river Elan has its source.

ELENNA (f)

see Elen.

ELENYDD (f)

see Elenid.

ELERA (f)

ELERI (f)

One of Brychan's daughters; the name of a river in Ceredigion.
Eleri Morgan and Eleri Siôn are television and radio broadcasters.

ELERYDD (m)

ELFAEL (m)

A district in the southern part of the old county of Radnorshire.

ELFAIR (f)

ELFED (m)

The Old Welsh name for the district around Leeds; also the bardic name of Elvet Lewis (1860–1953).

ELFEDAN (m)

ELFFIN (m) ELPHIN (m)

In Welsh legend, the baby Taliesin was rescued by Elffin ap Gwyddno. The legend is featured in the novel by Thomas Love Peacock (1785–1866), *The Misfortunes of Elphin* (1829).

ELFEIRA (f)

ELFODD (m) ELFODDW (m)

The bishop of Bangor who adopted the Roman way of calculating Easter Sunday.

ELFODDW (m)

see Elfodd.

ELFRYN (m)

ael, a brow + *bryn*, a hill.

ELFRYS (f)

ELFYN (m)

The bardic name of Robert Owen Hughes (1858–1919); Elfyn Llwyd is a Plaid Cymru MP.

E

ELGAN (m)

Elgan Rees played rugby for Wales in the 1970s and 1980s.

ELHAEARN (m)

see Aelhaearn.

ELI (m)

ELIAN (m)

An early saint.

ELIDR (m) ELYDR (m) ELIDYR (m)

The father of Llywarch Hen. Elidr Sais was a poet who lived in Anglesey in the 12th century.

ELIDYR (m)

see Elidr.

ELIN (f)

perhaps a diminutive form of Elinor.
Elin Jones is a Plaid Cymru member of the National Assembly.

ELINA (f)

See Elen.

ELINDER (f)

ELINOR (f)

Eleanor.
Elinor Bennett is a renowned harpist.

ELINWEN (f)

ELINWY (f)

ELIS (m)

Elias.
Lord Dafydd Elis-Thomas, formerly a Plaid Cymru MP, is Presiding Officer of the National Assembly for Wales.

ELISABETH (f)

Elizabeth.

ELISAWNDR (m)

Alexander.

ELISEDD (m)

The great-grandfather of Cyngen, who defended Powys from the Norman invaders in the 11th century.

ELISEG (m) ELYSTEG (f)

The king of Powys in the 9th century.

ELISSA (f)

ELISSOD (f)

a pet form of Elisabeth.

ELLI (f)

A 6th-century saint, one of the daughters of Brychan Brycheiniog, who is associated with Llanelli; her feast-day is 23 January.

ELLIW (f)

from *lliw*, colour.

ELONWY (f)

ELORA (f)

ELPHIN (m)

see Elffin.

ELUNED (f) EILUNED (f) LUNED (f)

Lynette (f).
The name of a woman in the tale of the Lady of the Fountain; Eluned Morgan (1870–1938) was a writer and early feminist. Eluned Morgan was a Labour member of the European Parliament from 1994 to 2009.

ELSYN (m)

a diminutive form of Elis.

ELUNIS (f)

ELUSEN (m)

charity.

ELWEN (f)

see Elwyn.

ELWENA (f)

ELWY (m)

A river in Denbighshire; the town of St. Asaph is known in Welsh as Llanelwy.

ELWYN (m) ELWEN (f)

A form of Alwyn.

ELYDR (m)

see Elidr.

ELYSTAN (m)

from Athelstan or Edelstan (Old English) Elystan Morgan was Labour MP for Cardiganshire (1966–74).

ELYSTEG (f)

see Eliseg.

EMLYN (m)

Aemilianus (Latin).
The town of Newcastle Emlyn (Castellnewydd Emlyn) is in Carmarthenshire. Emlyn Williams (1905–87) was an eminent playwright and actor.

EMRYS (m)

Ambrosius (Latin), Ambrose.
Emrys ap Iwan was the pseudonym of the patriotic writer Robert Ambrose Jones (1848–1906).

EMSYL (f)

EMWNT (m)

see Edmwnd.

EMYR (m)

A form of Ynyr.
Emyr Humphreys is a distinguished Welsh prose-writer. Emyr Lewis played rugby for Wales in the 1990s.

ENA (f)

see Enid.

E

ENDAF (m)

from *daf*, good.
Endaf Emlyn is a Welsh composer and film-maker.

ENDDWYN (m) ENDEWYN (m)

from *dwyn*, pleasant.

ENDEWYN (m)

see Enddwyn.

ENEIRETH (f)

ENFAIL (f)

see Onfael.

ENFYS (f) ENFYSG (f)

a rainbow.

ENFYSG (f)

see Enfys.

ENIAWN (f)

see Einion.

ENID (f) ENIDA (f) ENA (f)

The daughter of Yniwl Iarll and wife of Geraint, one of Arthur's knights; despite mistreatment by her husband, she remains faithful to him.

ENIDA (f)

see Enid.

ENIDWEN (f)

ENLLI (m)

The Welsh name for the island of Bardsey.

ENNIS (f)

ENOC (m)

Enoch.

ENSYL (m)

ENYDD (f)

EOS (f)

a nightingale.

ERCWLF (m)

Hercules.

ERDDYN (m)

ERF (m)

A warrior described in *Y Gododdin* as 'a bull of battle'.

ERFYL (m)

The village of Llanerfyl is in Powys; Gwyn Erfyl (1924–2007) was a distinguished broadcaster.

ERIN (f) ERYN (f) ERINA (f)

A Welsh name for Ireland.

ERINA (f)

see Erin.

ERMIN (m)

from Latin, *hermini*, lordly.

ERNIS (m)

ERNIS (m)

EROF (m)

Herod (Hebrew).

ERTHGI (m)

see Erthig.

ERTHIG (m) ERTHGI (m)

from *arth*, a bear.
A river in Ceredigion.

ERWYD (m)

ERYL (mf) ERYLA (f) ERYLYS (f)

a lookout.

ERYLA (f)

see Eryl.

ERYLLT (m)

ERYLYS (f)

see Eryl.

ERYN (f)

see Erin.

ERYRI (m)

abode of eagles.
The Welsh name for Snowdonia.

ESGAIRWYN (m)

ESSYLLT (f)

see Esyllt.

ESTYN (m)

ESWEN (f)

from *esgwyn*, strength.

ESYLLT (f) ESSYLLT (f)

The lover of Trystan; she is also known as Iseult and Isolde, as in Wagner's opera, *Tristan und Isolde*.

ETHELLT (f)

perhaps a form of Esyllt, influenced by Ethel.

ETHELWEN (f)

ETHNI (f)

The name of a heroine in Irish mythology, which has been adopted by the Welsh.

EUDAF (m)

EUDDOGWY (m)

A 6th-century saint whose feast-day is 2 July.

EUGRAD (m)

An early saint and brother of Gildas. Llaneugrad is in Anglesey.

E

EULAD (m)

EULANWY (mf)

EULFWYN (f)

from *mwyn*, gentle.

EUNYDD (m)

EURDDOLEN (f)

aur, gold + *dolen*, a link.

EURDDYLED (f)

EURDYDD (f)

EUREM (f)

EURFIN (m)

EURFRON (f)

aur, gold + *bron*, a breast.

EURFRYN (m)

aur, gold + *bryn*, a hill.

EURFYL (m)

from *aur*, gold.
a variant of Erfyl.

EURGAIN (mf)

aur, gold + *cain*, beautiful.
The village of Llaneurgain (Northop) is
in Flintshire.

EURIANA (f)

see Eurion.

EURIG (m)

see Eirig.

EURION (m) EURIONA (f) EURIANA (f)

from *aur*, gold.

EURIONA (f)

see Eurion.

EURLIW (mf)

aur, gold + *lliw*, colour.

EUROF (m)

aur, gold + *gof*, a smith.

EUROLWYN (f)

aur, gold + *olwyn*, a wheel.
A character in the tale of Culhwch and
Olwen.

EURON (f)

from *aur*, gold.
The name of a woman loved by the poet
Iolo Goch in the 14th century.

**EUROS (m) EUROSWY (f)
EUROSWEN (f)**

from *aur*, gold.
Euros Bowen (1904–88) was a distinguished Welsh poet.

EUROSWEN (f)

see Euros.

46

EUROSWYDD (m)

The father of Efnisien and Nisien in the Mabinogion.

EURWEL (m)

EURWEN (f) EURWYN (m)

aur, gold + *gwen, gwyn*, white.

EURWYN (m)

see Eurwen.

EURYDD (m)

EURYL (f)

from *aur*, gold + Irish *geal*, bright.

EURYN (m)

a gold trinket.

EURYS (mf)

from *aur*, gold.

EWIG (f)

a roe deer.

EWYNDON (m)

ewyn, foam + *don*, a wave.

F

FALEIRY (f)

Valerie.

FALMAI (f)

Valmai.

FANW (f)

a diminutive form of Myfanwy.

FFAGAN (m)

An early saint whose name is remembered in the place-name St. Fagans, near Cardiff, where the Museum of Welsh Life is situated.

FFESTIN (m)

FFION (f) FFIONA (f)

from Gaelic, *fionn*, fair or white.
Ffion Jenkins is the wife of former.
Conservative leader William Hague.

FFIONA (f)

see Ffion.

FFLUR (f)

flowers.
The daughter of Gweirydd ap Seisyllt. The church of Strata Florida in Ceredigion is known in Welsh as Ystrad Fflur.

FFOLANT (mf)

Valentine.

FFOWC (m)

Foulke.
Islwyn Ffowc Elis (1924–2004) was a distinguished novelist.

FFRAID (f)

Bridget.
The saint of this name has churches in many parts of Wales.

FFRANC (m)

Frank, a diminutive form of Francis.

FFRANCON (m)

The valley of Nant Ffrancon is in Gwynedd.

FFRANSIS (m)

Francis.

FFREDWYN (m)

FFREUER (f)

The sister of Heledd, princess of Powys.

FFUONWEN (f)

FIOLED (f)

Violet.

FROHAWCH (m)

FYCHAN (m)

small or younger.
This name has been anglicized as Vaughan.

G

GAENOR (f) GEINOR (f)

a form of Gwenhwyfar.

GAFIN (m) GAFYN (m)

Gavin.

GAFRAN (m)

GAFYN (m)

see Gafin.

GAIANYDD (m)

GANDWY (m)

GARAN (m)

a heron.
Garan Rhys Evans has played rugby for Wales.

GAREL (m)

Professor Garel Rhys is a distinguished academic.

GAREM (m)

GARETH (mf)

perhaps a form of Geraint or from *gwaraidd*, civilized; the name is usually masculine and only rarely feminine. Gareth Edwards is one of the finest rugby-players ever produced in Wales.

GARIN (m)

Garin Jenkins has played rugby for Wales.

GARMON (m)

The Welsh form of Germanus (Latin), the saint who came to Britain to defend Roman civilization against Vortigern (Gwrtheyrn) in the 5th century; he is the patron saint of Powys. Huw Garmon played the part of Hedd Wyn in the Oscar-nominated film.

GARN (m)

GARNON (m)

GAROD (m)

Gerald, Gerard, Giraldus (Latin).

GARTH (m)

a hill or promontory, closed space or rough land.
The Garth is a mountain to the north of Cardiff.

GARWEN (f)

GARWYN (m)

Cynan Garwyn was the king of Powys and patron of the poet Taliesin in the 6th century.

GAWAIN (m) GAWEN (m)

Gavin.
A hero of Arthurian romance.

GAWEN (m)

see Gawain.

GEINOR (f)

see Gaenor.

GELER (m)

GELLAN (m)

A poet and harpist in the 11th century.

GENERYS (f)

The woman loved by the poet-prince Hywel ab Owain Gwynedd in the 12th century.

GERAINT (m) GEREINT (m)

The hero in the medieval tale of Geraint and Enid. Geraint Evans (1922–92) was a famous opera-singer.

GERALLT (m)

Gerald, Gerard, Giraldus (Latin).
Giraldus Cambrensis (Gerald the Welshman, c. 1146–1223) is known in Welsh as Gerallt Gymro; R. Gerallt Jones (1934–99) was a distinguished writer and Gerallt Lloyd Owen is one of the best contemporary Welsh poets.

GEREINT (m)

see Geraint.

GERRAN (m)

GERSON (f)

GERWYN (m)

garw, rough + *gwyn*, white.
One of the sons of Brychan Brycheiniog.

GETHAN (m)

see Gethin.

GETHEN (m)

see Gethin.

GETHIN (m) GETHAN (m) GETHEN (m)

dusky.
Rhys Gethin was one of Owain Glyndwr's lieutenants.

GETTA (f)

GEUFRONWEN (f)

GILDAS (m)

A contemporary of Dewi Sant (St. David).

GILFAETHWY (m)

The son of Dôn, in the tale of Math fab Mathonwy in the Mabinogion.

GIRIOEL (m)

GLADYS (f)

see Gwladys.

GLAIN (f)

a jewel.

GLANDEG (mf)

glân, clean + *teg*, fair.

G

GLANDON (m)

GLANFFRWD (m)

glan, a bank + *ffrwd*, a stream.
The bardic name of William Thomas (1843–90), author of a celebrated history of Llanwynno.

GLANFYN (m)

GLANLI (m)

GLANMOR (m)

glan, bank + *mor*, great or *môr*, sea.
Glanmor Williams (1920–2005) was a distinguished Welsh historian.

GLANRUDD (f)

GLASFRYN (m)

GLASLYN (f)

Aberglaslyn is a well-known beauty-spot in Gwynedd.

GLASNANT (m)

glas, blue or grey + *nant*, a stream.

GLASYNYS (m)

glas, blue or grey + *ynys*, an island.
Glasynys was the bardic name of the writer Owen Wynne Jones (1828–70).

GLENDA (f)

This name could be of American, rather than Welsh, origin. Glenda Jackson, now a Labour MP, began her career as an actress.

GLENFIL (m)

GLENNA (f)

GLENWEN (f) GLENWYN (m)

GLENWYN (m)

see Glenwen.

GLENYDD (f)

GLENYS (f)

glân, clean, fair, holy.
Glenys Kinnock, the wife of the former Labour leader Neil Kinnock, was a Labour member of the European Parliament from 1994 to 2009.

GLESIG (f)

from *glas*, blue or fresh.

GLESNI (f)

from *glas*, blue or fresh.

GLWYS (f)

fair, beautiful, holy.

GLYN (m) GLYNNE (m)

a vale.
The dimunitive form of Glyndŵr. Glyn Jones (1905–95) was a distinguished writer in English.

GLYNA (f)

GLYNDŴR (m)

glyn, vale + *dŵr*, water.
Owain Glyndŵr, who rose against English rule in the early 15th century, is the national hero of the Welsh people.

GLYNETH (f)

GLYNGWYN (m)

glyn, a vale + *gwyn*, white.

GLYNIS (f) GLYNYS (f)

feminine forms of Glyn.
The name enjoyed a brief vogue during the film career of Glynis Johns.

GLYNNE (m)

see Glyn.

GLYNOG (m)

GLYNWEN (f)

GLYNYS (f)

see Glynis.

GLYTHEN (f) GLYTHIN (f)

GLYWYS (m)

Glywys was king of Glywysing (Glamorgan) in the 6th century.

GOEWIN (f)

see Goewyn.

GOEWYN (f) GOEWIN (f)

The maidservant of Math in the Mabinogion.

GOFANNON (m)

the Welsh name for Jupiter.
The god of blacksmiths and brother of Arianrhod in the Mabinogion.

GOLEUBRYD (f)

golau, light + *bryd*, countenance.

GOLEUDYDD (f)

golau, light + *dydd*, day.
The mother of the hero in the tale of Culhwch and Olwen.

GOLYSTAN (m)

A warrior who fell at the battle of Catraeth.

GOMERIAN (m)

from Gomer.
It was once believed that the Welsh were the descendants of Gomer, the grandson of Noah.

GORONW (m)

see Goronwy.

GORONWY (m) GORONW (m) GRONW (m) GRONO (m) RONW (m)

In the Mabinogion Blodeuwedd spends a night with Gronw Pebr, lord of Penllyn, and for her infidelity is changed into an owl. Goronwy Owen (1723–69) was one of the most distinguished Welsh poets of the 18th century.

G

GORTHYN (m)

A warrior praised for his generosity in *Y Gododdin*.

GORWEL (m)

horizon.

GORWEN (f)

GRAID (m)

heat, ardour.
A warrior praised for his courage in *Y Gododdin*.

GREDIFAEL (m)

A saint to whom the church at Penmynydd in Anglesey is dedicated.

GREIDAWL (m)

from *graid*, heat or ardour.
The father of Gwythyr, who has to fight Gwyn ap Nudd in order to win the hand of Creuddylad, in the tale of Culhwch and Olwen.

GRENIGWEN (f)

GRIFF (m) GRUFF (m)

A diminutive form of Griffith or Gruffydd; Gruff Rhys is lead-singer with the Welsh band Super Furry Animals.

GRIFFRI (m)

GRIGOR (m)

Gregory.

GRISIAL (f)

crystal.

GRONGAR (m)

GRONO (m)

see Goronwy.

GRONW (m)

see Goronwy.

GRUFF (m)

see Griff.

GRUFFUDD (m) GRUFFYDD (m)

from Griphuid, *grip*, strong + *udd*, lord
Many of the princes and kings of Gwynedd bore this name, e.g. Gruffudd ap Cynan (c.1055–1137) and Gruffudd ap Llywelyn (d.1063). The name is anglicized as Griffith.

GRUFFYDD (m)

see Gruffudd.

GRUG (f)

heather.

GRUGWYN (m)

grug, heather + *gwyn*, white.

GURNOSWEN (f)

GUTO (m)

a pet form of Gruffudd.
Guto Nyth Bran (Griffith Morgan, 1700–37) was a famous runner; Guy Fawkes is known in Welsh as Guto Ffowc. Guto Harri is a journalist and broadcaster.

GUTUN (m) GUTYN (m)

Pet forms of Gruffydd.
Gutun Owain was a famous poet in the 15th century.

GUTYN (m)

see Gutun.

GWAEDNERTH (m)

gwaed, blood + *nerth*, strength.
One of the warriors celebrated in *Y Gododdin*

GWAENUS (m)

GWAENYDD (m)

see Gweinydd.

GWAIR (f)

hay.

GWALCHMAI (m)

gwalch, a falcon + *Mai*, May.
Gwalchmai ap Meilyr was a court poet in the 12th century. Gwalchmai is a village in Anglesey.

GWALIA (f)

The Latin name for Wales.

GWALLAWG (m) GWALLOG (m)

A king to whom Taliesin addressed poems in the 6th century.

GWALLOG (m)

see Gwallawg.

GWALLTER (m)

Walter.
Gwallter Mechain was the bardic name of Walter Davies (1761–1849).

GWANWYN (m)

Spring.

GWARNANT (m)

GWARTHEN (m)

An early saint, one of the founders of the monastery at Bangor Iscoed (Bangor-on-Dee) in Flintshire.

GWARWEN (f)

gwar, nape + *gwen*, white.

GWATCYN (m)

see Watcyn.

GWAUN (m)

a heath.

GWAUNLI (f)

GWAWL (mf)

light.
The man whom Rhiannon must marry against her wishes, in the Mabinogion.

GWAWR (f)

dawn.
The daughter of Brychan and mother of Llywarch Hen.

G

GWAWRDDUR (m)

One of the warriors of whom it is said in *Y Gododdin*, 'Although they were slain, they slew; not one returned to his homeland'.

GWAWRDDYDD (f)

gwawr, dawn + *dydd*, day.

GWAWRWEN (f)

gwawr, dawn + *gwen*, white.

GWEFRIG (m)

A stream in Powys, sometimes called the Chwefri.

GWEFRWAWR (m)

A warrior described in *Y Gododdin* as 'a wolf in his fury'.

GWEINYDD (m)

a servant.

GWAUNYDD (m)

GWEIRFYL (f)

see Gwerfyl.

GWEIRYDD (m)

Gweirydd ap Rhys was the bardic name of the writer Robert John Pryse (1807–89).

GWEIRYL (f)

see Gwerfyl.

GWELO (f)

GWEN (f)

white, fair, holy, blessed.
Perhaps an abbreviation of Gwenhwyfar or Gwenllian. One of Brychan's daughters was called thus.

GWÊN (m)

The last of the twenty-four sons of Llywarch Hen.

GWENABWY (m) GWERNABWY (m)

A warrior described in *Y Gododdin* as 'a prince amid the bloodshed'. In Welsh legend, the Eagle of Gwernabwy was reputed to be one of 'the Ancients of the World'.

GWENALLT (m)

The poet David Gwenallt Jones (1899–1968) took his middle name from Alltwen near Pontardawe in the Swansea Valley.

GWENANT (f)

see Gwynant.

GWENAU (m)

GWENAWEN (f)

GWENDA (f)

gwen, white + *da*, good.
perhaps a dimunitive form of Gwendolen.

GWENDDOLAU (m)

A chieftain of the Coeling family in the north of Britain in the 6th century.

GWENDDYDD (f)

gwen, white + *dydd*, day.

GWENDOLEN (f) GWENDOLENA (f) GWENDOLYN (f)

gwen, white + *dolen*, a link.
perhaps a form of Gwenddoleu.

GWENDOLENA (f)

see Gwendolen.

GWENDOLYN (f)

see Gwendolen.

GWENDRAETH (f) GWYNDRAETH (m) WYNDRAETH (m)

The name of two rivers in Carmarthenshire.

GWENER (f)

The Welsh for Venus and Friday.

GWENEURYS (f)

GWENFAIR

gwen, blessèd + *Mair*, Mary.

GWENFFRWD (f)

gwen, white + *ffrwd*, a stream.

GWENFOR (f)

gwen, white + *mawr*, great.

GWENFREWI (f)

Winifred (Old English).
A 7th-century saint associated with

north-east Wales; her feast-day is 3 November.

GWENFRON (f)

gwen, white + *bron*, breast.

GWENFYDD (f) GWENFUDD (f)

GWENFYL (f)

GWENHWYFAR (f) GWENIFER (f)

Guinevere, Jennifer.
The wife of Arthur.

GWENID (m)

GWENIFER (f)

see Gwenhwyfar.

GWENITH (f)

wheat.

GWENLAIS (f)

GWENLLI (f)

GWENLLIAN (f)

gwen, white + *lliant*, a stream.
In the 12th century Gwenllian, mother of the Lord Rhys, led an attack on the Normans near Cydweli.

GWENLLIANT (f)

A character in the tale of Culhwch and Olwen.

G

GWENLLIW (f)

gwen, white + *lliw*, colour.

GWENLYN (mf)

Gwenlyn Parry (1932–91) was a distinguished Welsh playwright.

GWENNAN (f)

from *gwen*, blessèd.

GWENNANT (f)

gwen, white + *nant*, a stream.

GWENNAUL (f)

GWENNO (f)

a dimunitive form of Gwen.

GWENNOL (f)

a swallow.

GWENNYS (f)

GWENOG (f)

A saint commemorated at Llanwenog in Ceredigion.

GWENOGFRYN (m) GWYNOGFRYN (m)

John Gwenogvryn Evans (1852–1930) was a distinguished Welsh scholar.

GWENONWY (f)

The daughter of Ifor Hael, patron of Dafydd ap Gwilym.

GWENT (m)

A region and later a county in southeast Wales.

GWENWYNWYN (m)

Lord of Powys in the 13th century.

GWENYNEN (f)

a bee.
The philanthropist Lady Llanover (1802–96) was known as Gwenynen Gwent.

GWERFUL (f)

see Gwerfyl.

GWERFYL (f) GWERFUL (f) GWEIRFYL (f) GWEIRYL (f)

A woman loved by the poet Hywel ab Owain Gwynedd in the 12th century. Gwerfyl Pierce Jones was Director of the Welsh Books Council from 1987 to 2009.

GWERN (m) GWERNFYL (f)

an alder.
The son of Branwen and Matholwch in the Mabinogion.

GWERNABWY (m)

see Gwenabwy.

GWERNAN (f)

see Gwernen.

GWERNEN (f) GWERNAN (f)

One of the daughters of Dôn.

GWERNFAB (m)

son of Gwern.

GWERNFYL (f)
see Gwern.

GWERNOS (m)

GWERNYDD (m)

GWERYSTAN (m)

GWESTYL (m)

GWESTYR (m)

GWESYN (m)

A river in Powys on which the village of Abergwesyn stands.

GWEURIL (m)

GWGAN (m)

Gwgan fab Meurig was king of Ceredigion in the 9th century.

GWGON (m)

A poet who flourished in the 13th century.

GWILI (m)

A river in Carmarthenshire and the bardic name of John Jenkins (1872–1936).

GWILLIAM (m)

John Gwilliam captained the Welsh rugby union team to two Grand Slams in 1950 and 1952.

GWILMA (m)

GWILMAI (m)

GWILYM (m)
William.
Gwilym Hiraethog was the bardic name of William Rees (1802–83), writer and political leader.

GWION (m)

The name given to Taliesin in his youth by his mother, Ceridwen, in the Mabinogion.

GWLADUS (f)

see Gwladys.

GWLADYS (f) GWLADUS (f) GWLADWEN (f)

perhaps the feminine form of Gwledig, a ruler.
Gwladus Ddu was the daughter of Llywelyn Fawr, king of Gwynedd, in the 13th century.

GWLGED (m)

A warrior praised for his valour in *Y Gododdin*.

GWLITHEN (f) GWLITHYN (m)

a dewdrop.

GWLITHYN (mf)

see Gwlithen.

GWRGAN (m)

gwr, a man + *can*, bright.
Gwrgan ap Bleddyn was a prince in mid-Wales in the 11th century.

GWRGANT (m)

Gwrgant ab Ithel was a prince of Glamorgan in the 10th century.

GWRGENAU (m)

gwr, a man + *cenau*, a whelp.

GWRGI (m)

gwr, a man + *ci*, a dog.

GWRHAFAL (m)

A warrior commemorated in *Y Gododdin*.

GWRI (m)

The name given to Pryderi when he was lost, in the Mabinogion.

GWRIAD (m)

A warrior praised for his valour in *Y Gododdin*.

GWRIEN (m)

One of the warriors who fell at the battle of Catraeth.

GWRIL (m)

GWRION (m)

another name for Gwydion.

GWRLAIS (m)

gwr, a man + *llais*, a voice.

GWRNERTH (m)

gwr, a man + *nerth*, strength.

GWRON (m)

a hero.

GWRTHEFR (m)

GWRTHEYRN (m)

A British ruler in the 5th century who was blamed for allowing the English to enter Britain; he is known in English as Vortigern.

GWRWELLING (m)

One of the warriors who fell at the battle of Catraeth.

GWYAR (m)

GWYDDELAN (f)

from *Gwyddel*, an Irishman + *an*, suffix
An early saint commemorated at Dolwyddelan in Gwynedd.

GWYDDERIG (m)

A river in Powys and Carmarthenshire.

GWYDDFID (f)

honeysuckle.

GWYDDIEN (m)

A warrior praised for his prowess with a spear in *Y Gododdin*.

GWYDDNO (m)

Gwyddno Garanhir was the ruler of Cantre'r Gwaelod, the drowned kingdom under the waters of what is today Cardigan Bay.

GWYDDON (m)

a philosopher.

GWYDION (m)

The magician who created Blodeuwedd out of flowers, in the Mabinogion. The Milky Way is known in Welsh as Caer Gwydion.

GWYDOL (m)

from *gwyd*, zest.

GWYDRIM (m)

GWYDYR (m)

GWYLAN (f)

a seagull.

GWYLFA (mf)

a watching-place.

GWYLFAI (mf)

gwyl, a festival + *Mai*, May.

GWYLLYN (m)

one of the first names of the actor Glenn Ford.

GWYLON (m)

gwyl, a festival.

GWYN (m)

white, blessèd, fair.
Gwyn ap Nudd was the king of Annwn, the Otherworld.

GWYNALLT (m)

gwyn, white + *allt*, a hill.

GWYNANT (m) GWENANT (f)

gwyn or *gwen*, white + *nant*, a stream.

GWYNDAF (m)

An early saint.
Gwyndaf Evans has enjoyed a highly successful career as a rally driver.

GWYNDON (m)

GWYNDRAETH (m)

See Gwendraeth.

GWYNDUD (m)

GWYNDWR (m)

GWYNEDD (m)

The powerbase and last stronghold of the native Welsh Princes. Now a county in north-west Wales.

GWYNEIRA (f)

gwyn, white + *eira*, snow.

GWYNEIRYS (f)

GWYNETH (f)

gwyn, white + *geneth*, a girl.
or from Gwynedd or *gwynaeth*, felicity, bliss.
Gwyneth Paltrow is an American actress.

GWYNFAI (m)

GWYNFI (m)

A river in Neath Port Talbot.

GWYNFIL (m)

A parish in Ceredigion.

GWYNFOR (m)

gwyn, white + *mawr*, great.
Gwynfor Evans (1912–2005) was president of Plaid Cymru from 1945 to 1981 and the party's first M.P.; he was elected to represent Carmarthenshire in 1966.

GWYNFRYN (m)

gwyn, white + *bryn*, a hill.
Hywel Gwynfryn is a popular broadcaster.

GWYNFYDD (m)

GWYNHAF (m)

GWYNHEFIN (m)

GWYNLAIS

gwyn, white + *clais*, a stream.
A stream near Tongwynlais to the north of Cardiff.

GWYNLI (m)

GWYNLLIW (m)

A 5th-century saint who became king of Gwynllwg in Gwent; he was also known as Woollo.

GWYNN (m)

see Gwyn

GWYNNE (m)

see Gwyn.

GWYNNO (m)

A saint who is commemorated at Llanwynno in Rhondda Cynon Taff.

GWYNOGFRYN (m)

see Gwenogfryn.

GWYNORA (f)

see Gwynoro.

GWYNORO (m) GWYNORA (f)

One of the five saints of Llanpumsaint in Carmarthenshire.

GWYNRUDD (m)

GWYNSUL (m)

GWYRFAB (m)

son of Gower.
The pseudonym of the poet Harri Webb (1920–94).

GWYRFAI (m)

A river in Gwynedd.

GWYROSYDD (m)

The bardic name of Daniel James (1847–1920).

GWYTHER (m)

see Gwythyr.

GWYRTHYFER (m)

GWYTHYR (m) GWYTHER (m) GWYTHERIN (m)

a victor.
A character in the tale of Culhwch and Olwen.

GWYTHERIN (m)

see Gwythyr.

H

HAF (f)

summer.

HAFESB (m)

Aberhafesb is a village in Powys.

HAFGAN (m)

haf, summer + *gân*, a song.
Hafgan, in Welsh myth, was king of the Underworld.

HAFINA (f)

a dimunitive form of Haf.
Hafina Clwyd is a journalist and broadcaster.

HAFREN (f)

from Latin, Sabrina, the river-goddess. The Welsh name for the river Severn.

HAFWEN (f) HAFWYN (m)

haf, summer + *gwen* and *gwyn*, fair.

HAFWYN (m)

see Hafwen.

HAIDDWEN (f)

HARRI (m)

from Latin, Henricus.
Harry, a diminutive form of Harold.
Harri Webb (1920–94) was a popular patriotic poet.

HAUROL (f)

HAWEN (f)

A river near Llangrannog in Ceredigion.

HAWIS (f)

see Hawys.

HAWYS (f) HAWIS (f)

A woman loved by the poet Hywel ab Owain Gwynedd in the 12th century.

HAWYSTL (f)

An early saint, the daughter of Brychan.

HEDD

peace.
Hedd Wyn was the bardic name of Ellis Humphrey Evans (1887–1917), who won the Chair at the Birkenhead National Eisteddfod in 1917 but was killed in the battle for Pilkem Ridge before the ceremony.

HEDDUS (m)

see Heddys.

HEDDWEL (m)

HEDDWEN (f)

see Heddwyn.

HEDDWYN (m) HEDDWEN (f)

hedd, peace + *gwyn*, blessèd.

HEDDYR (f)

Heather.

HEDDYS (f) HEDDUS (m)

HEDYDD (mf)

a skylark.

HEFEYDD (m)

Hefeydd Hen is the father of Rhiannon in the Mabinogion.

HEFIN (m) HEFINA (f)

summery
John Hefin is a distinguished film-maker.

HEFINA (f)

see Hefin.

HEIDDWYN (m)

HEILIN (m)

from *hael*, generous.

HEILYN (m)

a pourer of wine.
Heilyn fab Gwyn Hen, in the Mabinogion, was one of the seven who survived the campaign in Ireland when Brân went to rescue Bendigeidfran.

HEINI (m)

sprightly, fit.

Heini fab Nwython was one of the warriors celebrated in *Y Gododdin*. Heini Gruffudd is a prolific Welsh writer.

HEININ (m)

A poet who features in the tale of Taliesin.

HELEDD (f)

The sister of Cynddylan, prince of Powys in the 7th century, who mourns her brother's death in a series of poems which include '*Stafell Cynddylan*' (The Hall of Cynddylan). Heledd Cynwal is a television presenter. The Hebrides are known in Welsh as Ynysoedd Heledd.

HELENA (f)

HELYGEN (m)

The village of Llanfihangel Helygen is in Powys.

HENNIN (m)

HERGEST (m)

A house on the border of Powys and Herefordshire where an important manuscript, The Red Book of Hergest, was once kept.

HEULFRYN (m)

haul, sun + *bryn*, a hill.

HEULWEN (f) HEULWYN (m)

sunshine.

HEULWYN (m)

see Heulwen.

HEULYN (mf)

a ray of sunshine.

HEW (m)

see Huw.

HININ (m)

A poet in the late 14th century.

HIRAEL (mf) HIRAL (mf)

hir, long + *ael*, brow.

HIRAETHOG (m)

A district in Denbighshire. Gruffudd Hiraethog was a major Welsh poet in the 16th century.

HIRAL (f)

see Hirael.

HIRELGAS (m)

The son of Caswallon who, according to Geoffrey of Monmouth, was killed by Cuhelyn, the son of Afarwy.

HIRWAENA (f)

HIRWEN (f)

hir, long + *gwen*, white.

HOEN (f)

HOPCYN (m)

Hopkin.

HOWEL (m)

see Hywel.

HUAIL (m)

Huail son of Caw is described in the Triads as one of 'the Three Battle-diademed Men of the Isle of Britain'.

HUANA (f)

HUNYDD (f)

A woman loved by the poet Hywel ab Owain Gwynedd in the 12th century.

HUW (m) HEW (m)

from Hugi (Old German).
Huw Llewelyn Davies is a popular sports commentator and broadcaster. Huw Edwards is a renowned television journalist and broadcaster.

HUWAN (m)
A diminutive form of Huw.

HUWCYN (m)

A diminutive form of Huw.

HWFA (m)

Hwfa Môn was the bardic name of Rowland Williams (1823–1905), a native of Rhos Trehwfa in Anglesey.

HWLCYN (m)

a pet form of Hywel.

HWMFFRE (m)

Humphrey
a variant of Wmffre.

HYDREF (f)

October, Autumn.

HYFAIDD (m)

A warrior of whom the author of *Y Gododdin* wrote, 'He will be praised while there is a minstrel'. It may be that the Welsh name for Radnor, Maesyfed, is derived from *maes*, a field + Hyfaidd.

HYLWEN (f)

HYWEL (m) HOWEL (m) HYWELA (f)

eminent.

Hywel Dda was the prince of Wales who, in the 10th century, codified the Welsh laws; Hywel ab Owain Gwynedd (fl. 1140–70) was a soldier and poet. Howel Harris (1714–73) was one of the leaders of the Methodist Revival in Wales.

HYWELA (f)

see Hywel.

HYWELFRYN (m)

HYWYN (m)

a diminutive form of Hywel.
One of the saints commemorated at Aberdaron in Gwynedd.

I

IAGO (m)
Jacob, James.

IANTO (m)
a diminutive form of Ifan, Ieuan or Iago.

IARLLES (f)
a countess
Dr William Price (1800–93) of Llantrisant
gave this name to his daughter.

IDANWEN (f)

IDDAWG (m)
A character in *The Dream of Rhonabwy*,
a tale preserved in the Red Book of
Hergest.

IDDIG (m)
One of the seven princes left to defend
the Island of the Mighty (Britain) when
Brân leaves for Ireland, in the
Mabinogion.

IDDON (m)

IDLOES (m)
A saint commemorated at Llanidloes in
Powys.

IDNERTH (m)
id, lord + *nerth*, strength.
The last bishop of Llanbadarn Fawr bore
this name.

IDNO (m)

IDRIS (m)
Cader Idris, a mountain in Meirionydd,
is supposed to be named after a giant of
this name. Idris Davies (1905–53) was a
poet of industrial south Wales.

IDRISYN (m)
a diminutive form of Idris.

IDWAL (m) IDWALLON (m)
id, lord + *gwal*, ruler
Idwal Foel was king of Gwynedd in the
10th century. Llyn Idwal is a lake in
Gwynedd. Idwal Jones (1895–1937) was
a writer who believed that the Welsh 'did
not take their humour seriously'.

IDWALLON (m)
see Idwal.

IDWEN (f) IDWENNA (f)

IEMWNT (m)
see Edmwnd.

IESTYN (m)
from Latin, Justinus.
Justin.
Iestyn ap Gwrgant was the last independent ruler of Glamorgan in the 11th century. Iestyn Garlick is a popular actor.
Iestyn Harris has played rugby union and
rugby league for Wales.

IEUAF (m)
youngest.

I

IEUAN (m)

from Latin, Iohannes.
John, Evan.
Ieuan Fardd was the bardic name of Evan
Evans (1731–88) and Ieuan Gwynedd that
of the writer Evan Jones (1820–52). Ieuan
Evans played rugby for Wales and the
British Lions during the 1980s and 1990s.

IFAN (m) IFANNA (f) IFANWY (f)

from Latin, Iohannes.
John, Evan.

IFANNA (f)

see Ifan.

IFANWY (f)

see Ifan.

IFER (m)

IFON (m) IFONA (f)

IFONA (f)

see Ifon.

IFOR (m)

from *iôr*, a lord.
Ivor.
Ifor Bach was a lord of upland
Glamorgan in the 12th century and Ifor
Hael a patron of the poet Dafydd ap
Gwilym in the 14th century. Ivor Novello
(1893–1951) was a celebrated man of the
theatre. Ifor Davies is a distinguished
Welsh painter.

IFRYN (m)

ILAN (m)

A saint commemorated at Eglwys Ilan, a
church on the hill known as Mynydd
Meio between Trefforest and Abertridwr,
to the north of Cardiff.

ILAR (mf)

from Latin, *hilarus*, cheerful.
Hilary.

ILID (f)

Julitta (Latin).
A saint of this name is commemorated at
Llanilid in the Vale of Glamorgan.

ILLTUD (m) ILLTYD (m)

A Breton saint who is reputed to have
invented the plough; he is commemorated at Llanilltud Fawr (Llantwit Major)
in the Vale of Glamorgan, where Dewi and
Gildas were his pupils.

ILLTYD (m)

see Illtud.

ILTRYD (f)

ILYAN (m)

INA (f)

INDEG (f)

One of Arthur's handmaidens in the tale
of Culhwch and Olwen.

INIGO (m)

from Latin, Ignatius.
The architect Inigo Jones (1573–1652)
was a native of Llanrwst in Denbighshire.

I

INIR (m)

see Ynyr.

INYR (m)

see Ynyr.

IOAN (m)

from Latin, Iohannes.
John.
Ioan Gruffydd is a popular actor.

IOLA (f)

see Iolo.

IOLO (m) IOLYN (m) IOLA (f)

dimunitive forms of Iorwerth.
Iolo Goch was a poet in the 14th century
and Iolo Morganwg was the bardic name
of Edward Williams (1747–1826), the antiquary who invented the Gorsedd of
Bards. Iola Gregory is a well-known television actress.

IOLYN (m)

see Iolo.

ION (m)

IONA (f)

a short form of Ionawr (January).
The island of Iona lies off the western
coast of Scotland.

IONAWR (f)

see Ionor.

IONOR (f) IONAWR (f)

January.

IONORON (m)

IONWEN (f)

see Iorwen.

IORATH (m)

a form of Iorwerth.
This name, as a surname, has been anglicized to Yorath. Terry Yorath played
for and managed the Welsh national football team.

IORWEN (f) IONWEN (f)

iôr, a lord + *gwen*, blessèd.

IORWERTH (m)

iôr, a lord + *gwerth*, worth.
It has sometimes been assumed that this
name is cognate with Edward, but it is
not. Iorwerth ap Bleddyn was a prince of
Powys in the 12th century; Iorwerth
Cyfeiliog Peate (1901–82) was the first
curator of the Welsh Folk Museum at St.
Fagans.

IORYS (m)

IOSEFF (m)

from Hebrew, may Jehovah add
Joseph.

IRFON (m)

A river near Builth on the banks of which
Llywelyn ap Gruffudd, the last prince of
independent Wales, was killed by the
Anglo-Normans on 11 December 1282.

IRWEDD (m)

IRWEN (f) IRWYN (m)

ir, green or fresh + *gwen*, white.

IRWYN (m)

see Irwen.

ISAG (m)

One of the warriors celebrated in *Y Gododdin*, of whom it is said, 'His sword rang in the heads of mothers'.

ISAN (m)

ISFAEL (m)

A 6th-century saint who is associated with Dyfed.

ISFOEL (m)

is, under + *moel*, a hill.

ISFRYN (m)

is, under + *bryn*, a hill.

ISGOED (m)

is, under + *coed*, a wood.

ISLAN (m)

ISLWYN (m)

is, under + *llwyn*, a grove.
The poet William Thomas (1832–78) was known by his bardic name, Islwyn.

ISLYN (m)

ISNANT (m)

is, under + *nant*, a stream.

ITHAEL (m)

see Ithel

ITHEFEN (f)

ITHEL (m) ITHELA (f) ITHAEL (m)

ith, lord + *hael*, generous.

ITHELA (f)

see Ithel.

ITHWEN (m)

IVOR (m)

see Ifor

IWAN (m)

a form of Ifan.
Dafydd Iwan is a patriotic folk-singer, politician and businessman; Iwan Thomas won a gold medal for Wales at the 1998 Commonwealth Games. Iwan Bala is a distinguished Welsh painter.

IWERYDD (m)

The Welsh name for the Atlantic ocean.

J

There is no J in the modern Welsh alphabet.

JAC (m)

Jack.

JOSEFF (m)

see Ioseff.

K

There is no K in the modern Welsh alphabet.

KEIDRYCH (m)

see Ceidrych.

KELT (m)

see Celt.

KYFFIN (m)

see Cyffin.

KYNFFIG (m)

see Cynffig.

KYNRIC (m)

see Cynfrig.

L

LANDEG (m)

a form of Glandeg.

LAWNSLOD (m)

One of Arthur's knights, a character invented by Chrétien de Troyes as Launcelot in the 12th century.

LENA (f)

LERI (f)

a diminutive form of Eleri, Teleri and Meleri.

LETYS (f)

Lettice, Letitia.

LEWIS (m)

see Lewys.

LEWSYN (m)

a diminutive form of Lewys.

LEWYS (m) LEWIS (m)

forms of Llywelyn.
Ludwig (German), Louis (French)
Lewis Glyn Cothi was a poet in the 15th century.
Lewis Jones (1897–1939) was a novelist and Communist leader in the Rhondda during the interwar years.

LIETHAN (m)

LIFRIS (m)

LILI (f)

a lily.

LILWEN (f)

lili, a lily + *gwen*, white.

LISA (f)

a diminutive form of Elisabeth.

LIWLI (f)

LIWSI (f)

Lucy.

LLACHAU (m) LLECHEU (m)

He is named in the Triads as one of the wealthiest men in the Isle of Britain.

LLANDIS (m).

LLAWDDEN (m)

A poet from Loughor in Glamorgan in the 15th century.

LLAWEN (m)

joyful, happy.
A saint commemorated at Llanllawen near Aberdaron in Gwynedd.

LLECHEU (m)

see Llachau.

LLECHID (f)

The village of Llanllechid, near Bethesda in Gwynedd, is named after a saint of this name.

LLEFELYS (m)

The king of France in the medieval tale of Lludd and Llefelys.

LLEISION (m)

Leyshon.

LLELO (m)

a diminutive form of Llywelyn.

LLEU (m)

light, fair one.
Lleu Llaw Gyffes, in the Mabinogion, is the son of Arianrhod; Gwydion provides him with a name, weapons and a wife, Blodeuwedd.

LLEUCU (f)

from *lleu*, light.
Lleucu Llwyd was loved by the poet Hywel ab Owain Gwynedd in the 12th century.

LLEUFER (m)

light, splendour.

LLEW (m)

a lion.
a pet form of Llewelyn.

LLEWELA (f)

see Llywel.

LLEWELFRYN (m)

LLEWELYN (m)

see Llywelyn.

LLIAN (f)

flaxen, linen.

LLIEDI (f)

A river in Carmarthenshire.

LLIF (m)

A warrior commemorated in *Y Gododdin*.

LLIFON (m)

A river in Gwynedd.

LLINOR (f)

LLINOS (f)

a linnet

LLIO (f)

a diminutive form of Gwenllian.
Llio Millward is a popular singer.

LLION (m)

caer, a fort + *legionum* (L), of the legions + suffix, *on*.
This name has nothing to do with Caerleon, in Gwent, which is known in Welsh as Caerllion. Llion Williams is a well-known television actor.

LLIOR (f)

LLIWEN (m)

L

LLUAN (f)

A saint commemorated at Llanlluan in Carmarthenshire

LLUDD (m)

The king of Britain in the medieval tale of Lludd and Llefelys

LLUDDOCAF (m)

LLUGAN (m)

LLUGWY (m)

LLUNGWYN (m)

The Welsh word for Whitsun Monday

LLUNWERTH (m)

llun, a form or shape + *gwerth*, value

LLUSTYN (m)

see Llystyn

LLWYD (m)

grey, holy
Lloyd, formerly Lhuyd, as in the name of Edward Lhuyd (1660?–1709), scientist and philologist

LLWYFO (m)

Llew Llwyfo was the bardic name of Lewis William Lewis (1831–1901).

LLYFNI (m)

A river in Gwynedd

LLYFNWY (m)

LLYNDAF (m)

LLYNFI (m)

A river near Bridgend which flows into the Ogwr

LLYNNOR (f)

see Llynor

LLYNOR (f) LLYNNOR (f)

LLŶR (m)

The father of Branwen and Brân (Bendigeidfran) in the Mabinogion; he is known in English as Lear. Leicester is known in Welsh as Caer Llŷr.

LLYSTYN (f) LLUSTYN (m)

LLYWARCH

llyw, a leader + *march*, a horse
Llywarch Hen was a British prince in the 6th century whose story was told in verse c. 850.

**LLYWEL (m) LLYWELA (f)
LLEWELA (f)**

A saint commemorated at Llywel in Powys; Llywela is Americanized to Louella.

LLYWELA (f)

see Llywel

LLYWELYDD (m)

LLYWELYN (m) LLEWELYN (m)

llyw, a leader + *eilyn*, attributes of Llywelyn ap Iorwerth (1173–1240), known as Llywelyn Fawr (The Great), was prince of Gwynedd; his grandson, Llywelyn ap Gruffudd, the last prince of independent Wales, was killed by the forces of Edward I on 11 December 1282. The name was anglicized by Shakespeare as Fluellen and later corrupted to Llewellyn.

LODES (f)

a maiden

LOIS (f)

from Greek, *Ioion,* highly desired female warrior
A biblical name that is growing in popularity in Wales

LONA (f)

a diminutive form of Maelona or Moelona

LORA (f)

Laura

LOWRI (f)

Laura
The mother of William Morgan, who translated the Bible into Welsh in 1588, bore this name.

LUC (m)

a biblical name, Luke

LUNED (f)

see Eluned

LYN (mf) LYNN (m) LYNNE (f)

diminutive forms of Llywelyn or Eluned

LYNDRUM (m)

LYNETH (f)

from Lynette (French), which derived from Eluned

LYNFA (f)

from *glyn*, a vale

LYNFEL (m)

LYNN (f)

see Lyn

LYNNE (f)

see Lyn

LYNWEN (f)

glyn, a vale + *gwen*, white

LYSOD (f)

a pet form of Elisabeth

M

MABEN (m)

see Mabon.

MABLI (f)

Mabel
Cefn Mabli is a mansion near Cardiff.

MABON (m) MABYN (m) MABEN (m)

The Celtic god of youth who was identified by the Romans with Apollo. William Abraham (1842–1922), M.P. for the Rhondda, was known by his eisteddfodic name, Mabon.

MABYN (m)

see Mabon.

MACHNO (m)

A river in Gwynedd. Penmachno is a village in the county.

MACHRETH (m)

A saint commemorated at Llanfachreth in Anglesey and in Meirionydd.

MACSEN (m)

from Latin, Magnus.
Macsen Wledig (Magnus Maximus) was emperor of Rome and the husband of Helen of the Hosts.

MADAWC (m)

see Madog.

MADLEN (f) MODLEN (f) MALEN (f)

from Hebrew, Magdalene.

MADOC (m)

see Madog.

MADOG (m) MADOC (m) MADAWC (m)

from *mad*, good.
A prince of Gwynedd who is reputed to have sailed across the Atlantic and discovered America in the 12th century; the traditional tale gave rise to belief in the existence of a tribe of Welsh-speaking Indians, the Mandans. Porthmadog, a town in Gwynedd, and nearby Tremadoc, was developed by William Alexander Maddocks (1773–1828). Philip Madoc is a well-known actor.

MADRON (f)

see Modron.

MADRUN (mf) MADRYN (mf)

The daughter of Gwrtheyr in the 5th century; Carn Madryn is a mountain in Llŷn.

MADRYN (f)

see Madrun.

MAEL (m)

a prince.

MAELAN (m)

from *mael*, a prince.

MAELDERW (m)

mael, a prince + *derw*, an oak.

MAELGAD (m)

mael, a prince + *cad*, a battle.

MAELGWN (m) MAELGWYN (f)

from *mael*, a prince.
Maelgwn Gwynedd was a British leader in the 6th century.

MAELGWYN (m)

see Maelgwn.

MAELIENYDD (m)

The northern part of the old county of Radnorshire.

MAELOG (m) MAELOGAN (m)

from *mael*, a prince.
The Maelogan is a stream in north-east Wales.

MAELOGAN (m)

see Maelog.

MAELON (m) MAELONA (f)

from *mael*, a prince.

MAELONA (f)

see Maelon.

MAELOR (m)

A district in Flintshire.

MAELORWEN (f)

Maelor + *gwen*, white or blessèd.

MAELRYS (m)

mael, a prince + *rhys*, rushing.

MAELWAS (m)

mael, a prince + *gwas*, a youth or servant
He abducted Gwenhwyfar in the Arthurian tale.

MAENGWYN (m)

maen, a stone + *gwyn*, white.

MAESMOR (m)

MAGDALEN (f)

Magdalene.

MAGLONA (f)

This name is associated with the town of Machynlleth in Powys, but this is an erroneous view attributable to the antiquary William Camden (1551–1623).

MAGWEN (f)

MAI (f)

May.

MAIR (f)

from Hebrew, a beloved child.
Mary.

M

MAIRWEN (f) MAIRWENA (f) MEIRWEN (f)

Mair + *gwen*, blessèd.

MALAN (f)
see Malen.

MALDWYN (m)

Baldwin (Old English).
The town of Montgomery is known in Welsh as Trefaldwyn.

MALEN (f) MALAN (f)

see Magdalen.

MALI (f)

a form of Mary and the equivalent of Molly.

MALLEN (f)

MALLT (f)

Matilda, Maude.

MALWYN (m)

MANAWYD (m)

see Manawydan.

MANAWYDAN (m) MANAWYD (m)

The son of Llŷr, brother of Brân (Bendigeidfran), in the Mabinogion.

MANLLWYD (m)

MANOD (mf)

A mountain in Meirionnydd.

MANON (f)

a paragon of beauty
Manon Rhys is a distinguished prose-writer.

MARARAD (f)

see Marared.

MARARED (f) MARARAD (f)

a form of Marged.

MARC (m)

Mark.

MARCHELL (f)

The mother of Brychan Brycheiniog.

MARCHLEW (m)

march, a horse + *llew*, a lion.

MARCHUDD (m)

march, a horse + *udd*, a lord.

MARCHWEITHIAN (m)

MARDY (m)

Anglicized form of Maerdy, a village in the Rhondda. T.I. Mardy Jones was Labour M.P. for Pontypridd (1922–31).

MARED (f)

a form of Marged.

MAREDUDD (m) MEREDYDD (mf) MERYDYDD (m)

mawr, great + *udd*, a lord.
The anglicized form Meredith is used as both a masculine and feminine name, especially in the USA.

MARGED (f) MARGRED (f)

a pearl.
Margaret.

MARGIAD (f)

a form of Marged, especially in north Wales.
Margiad Evans was the pseudonym of the writer Peggy Eileen Whistler (1909–58).

MARGRED (f)

see Marged.

MARI (f) MERI (f)

a variant of Mari.

MARIAN (f) MARION (f)

a diminutive form of Mari.
Marion Eames is a distinguished Welsh novelist.

MARION (f)

see Marian.

MARLAIS (m) MARLES (m)

mawr, big + *clais*, a stream.
The name of two rivers in Carmarthenshire.
Marlais was the middle name of the poet Dylan Thomas (1914–53).

MARLES (m)

see Marlais

MARLIS (f)

MARLYN (f)

MARNEL (f)

MARRO (m)

The father of one of the warriors slain at Catraeth.

MARSLI (f)

MARTEG (m)

a river in Powys

MARTYN (m)

from Latin, Martinus (Mars).
Martin.
Martyn Lewis is a popular broadcaster.
Martyn Williams has played rugby union for Wales and the British Lions.

MATH (m)

Math fab Mathonwy, lord of Gwynedd, was a magician who created Blodeuwedd out of flowers, as related in the Mabinogion.

MATHOLWCH (m)

The king of Ireland who married Branwen in the Mabinogion.

M

MATHONWY (m)

The father of Math in the Mabinogion.

MATHRAFAL (m)

The principal court of the rulers of Powys until the 13th century.

MATI (f)

MAWDWEN (f)

see Medwen.

MECHAIN (m)

A district of Powys.

MEDENI (f)

Medi, September + *geni*, to be born.

MEDI (f)

September.

MEDRAWD (m) MEDROD (m)

medd, to own + *rhawd*, a host.
One of Arthur's knights who is said to have died with him at the battle of Camlann.

MEDROD (m)

see Medrawd.

MEDWEN (f) MAWDWEN (f) MEDWENNA (f)

An early saint and companion of St. Patrick.

MEDWENNA (f)

see Medwen.

MEDWYN (m)

A saint whose feast-day is 1 January.

MEDYR (m)

MEFELDA (f)

MEFIN (mf)

from *Mehefin*, June.
Mefin Davies has played rugby union for Wales.

MEG (f)

see Megan.

MEGAN (f) MEG (f)

a form of Marged.
Megan Lloyd George (1902–66) was Liberal MP for Anglesey, 1929–51, and Labour MP for Carmarthen, 1957–66.

MEIC (m)

a diminutive form of Meical.
Meic Myngfras was the traditional ancestor of the rulers of Glyndyfrdwy in northern Powys. Meic Stevens is a popular singer and Meic Povey a distinguished actor and playwright.

MEICAL (m)

Michael.

MEIDRYM (m)

A village in Carmarthenshire.

MEIFYN(m)

MEIGANT(m)

MEILIR(m) MEILYR(m)

Meilyr Brydydd Hir was a poet in the 12th century.

MEILYG(m)

A character in the tale of Culhwch and Olwen.

MEILYR(m)

see Meilir.

MEILYS(mf)

A name popular in the old county of Montgomeryshire.

MEINIR(f)

a maiden.

MEINLYR(m)

MEINWEN(f)

main, slender + *gwen*, white.

MEIRA(f)

Myra.

MEIRCHION(m)

from *meirch*, horses.
Tremeirchion is a village in Flintshire.

MEIRIAN(f)

The antiquary Richard Morris (1703–79) of Anglesey gave this name to his daughter.

MEIRION(m) MEIRIONA(f)

The grandson of Cunedda, who gave his name to a part of Gwynedd which later became Meirionnydd (Merioneth).

MEIRIONA(f)

see Meirion.

MEIRIONWEN(f)

Meirion + *gwen*, white.

MEIRIS(f)

MEIROS(f)

MEIRWEN(f)

see Mairwen.

MEIRYS(f)

MEIWYN(m)

MELANGELL(f)

The daughter of Tudwal ap Ceredig; according to the traditional tale, she sheltered a hare from the hounds of Brochfael Ysgythrog and was known thereafter as the patron saint of small creatures. A church is dedicated to her at Llanfihangel-y-Pennant in the old county of Montgomeryshire and hares are known in Welsh as '*wyn Melangell*' (Melangell's lambs).

MELAR(m)

see Melor.

MELERI(f)

a form of Eleri.
She was the daughter of Brychan Brycheiniog and grandmother of Dewi (St. David).

M

MELFA(f)

MELFYDD(f)

MELFUDD(f)

MELFYN(m)

a form of Merfyn.

MELINA(f)

MELOR(m) MELAR(m)

variants of Meilyr.

MELWAS(m)

MEN(f)

a diminutive form of Menna.
A woman to whom the poet Eifion Wyn
(Eliseus Williams, 1867–1926) addressed
some of his poems.

MENAI(f)

The Menai Straits separate Anglesey
from the mainland of Gwynedd.

MENEIRA(f)

MENNA(f)

The woman loved by Alun Mabon in a
poem by John Ceiriog Hughes (1832–87);
Menna Elfyn is a contemporary poet.

MENW(f)

main, slender + *gwen*, white.

MERDDYN(m)

see Myrddin.

MEREDYDD(m)

see Maredudd.

MERERID(f) MERIERID(f)

A precious stone.
Forms of Marged.
Mererid Hopwood became the first
woman to win the Chair at the National
Eisteddfod at Denbigh in 2001.

MEREWENNA(f)

MERFYN(m)

Mervyn.
Merfyn Frych was king of Gwynedd in
the 9th century. Mervyn Davies played
rugby union for Wales and the British
Lions in the 1970s.

MERI(f)

see Mari.

MERIADEG(m)MERIADOG(m)

variants of Meredydd.

MERIADOG(m)

see Meriadeg.

MERIAN(f)

MERIEL(f)MERYL(f)MYRIEL(f)

from Irish, *muir*, the sea + *geal*, bright.

MERIERID(f)

see Mererid.

84

MERLYN (m)

see Myrddin.

MERLYS (f)

MERYDYDD (m)

see Maredudd.

MERYL (f)

see Meriel.
Meryl Streep is an American filmstar.

MEUDWEN (f)

meudwy, a hermit + *gwen*, blessèd.

MEUGAN (m)

A saint to whom the church at Llan-feugan in Powys is dedicated.

MEURIG (m)

from Latin, Mauricius.
Maurice (French).
A river in Ceredigion from which the village of Trefeurig takes its name.

MEURON (f)

MEURYN (m)

from *meiriol*, thaw or *euryn*, golden one
Meuryn was the bardic name of Robert John Rowlands (1880–1967).

MIALL (m)

David Miall Edwards (1873–1941) was a theologian and writer.

MINDWR (m)

MIHANGEL (m)

from Hebrew, like the Lord.
Michael.
Mihangel Morgan is a leading Welsh prose-writer.

MILWYN (m)

MINWEL (f)

MODLEN (f)

see Madlen.

MODRON (f) MADRON (m)

A Celtic goddess; the mother of Mabon in the tale of Culhwch and Olwen.

MODWEN (f) MODWENNA (f)

MODWENNA (f)

see Modwen.

MOEDDYN (m)

MOELFED (m)

MOELONA (f)

The pseudonym of the writer Elizabeth Mary Jones (1878–1953).

MOELWEN (f)

see Moelwyn.

MOELWYN (m) MOELWEN (f)

moel, a hill + *gwyn, gwen*, white.

MOI (m)

M

MOLD (f)

a diminutive form of Matilda.
This name has nothing to do with the town of Mold (Yr Wyddgrug) in Flintshire.

MÔN (m) MONA (f)

Anglesey.
The island is sometimes called 'Môn, mam Cymru' (Anglesey, the mother of Wales).

MONA (f)

see Môn.

MORDAF (m)

MORDANT (m)

MORDEYRN (m)

mawr, great + *teyrn*, a ruler.

MOREIDDIG (m)

MOREN (m)

A character mentioned in the tale of Culhwch and Olwen.

MORFA (f)

MORFAEL (m)

mawr, great + *mael*, a prince.

MORFEN (f)

MORFIN (m) MORFINA (f)

MORFINA (f)

see Morfin.

MORFORWYN (f)

a mermaid.

MORFRAN (m)

mor, great + *brân*, a crow.
The hideously ugly son of Tegid Foel and the goddess Ceridwen in the Mabinogion, is also called Afagddu.

MORFRYN (m)

MORFUDD (f)

The daughter of Urien Rheged in the tale of Culhwch and Olwen; also a fair-haired woman courted by the poet Dafydd ap Gwilym in the 14th century.

MORGAN (m)

môr, sea or *mawr*, great + *can*, bright or *cant*, circle.
Morgan, the son of Meurig ap Tewdrig, gave his name to Morgannwg (Glamorgan) in the 8th century. The name is common as a surname and is becoming increasingly popular as a first name.

MORGANT (m)

A king who fought with Urien Rheged.

MORIED (m)

A warrior whose courage is celebrated in *Y Gododdin*.

MORIEN (m)

môr, sea or *mawr*, great + *geni*, born.
One of the warriors who died in the battle of Catraeth; the journalist Owen Morgan (1836?–1921) was more generally known as Morien.

MORLAIS (m)

môr, sea or *mawr*, great + *llais*, a voice or *clais*, a ditch.

MORLAISYDD (m)

MORNANT (m)

MORUS (m) MORYS (m)

from Latin, Mauricius.
This name has been anglicized to Morris.

MORWEN (f) MORWENNA (f) MORWYN (m)

morwyn, a maid or *mawr*, great or *môr*, the sea or *mor*, so + *gwen*, white.

MORWENNA (f)

see Morwen.

MORWYN (m)

see Morwen.

MORWYTH (f)

MORYS (m)

see Morus.

MOSTYN (m)

A village near Flint in north-east Wales.

MWYNDEG (f)

mwyn, gentle + *teg*, fair.

MWYNLAN (f)

MWYNEN (f)

from *mwyn*, gentle.
A daughter of Brychan Brycheiniog.

MWYNWEN (f)

mwyn, gentle + *gwen*, white.

MYDDFAI (m)

A parish in Carmarthenshire famous for its association with a family of physicians.

MYFADNE (f)

MYFANWY (f)

from *manwy*, fine, rare.
The song 'Myfanwy' by Joseph Parry (1841–1903) made this name extremely popular.

MYFEDA (f)

MYFI (f) MYFINA (f)

diminutive forms of Myfanwy.

MYFINA (f)

see Myfi.

MYFONA (f)

MYFYR (m)

a muse, to study.

MYLLIN (m)

A saint to whom the church at Llanfyllin in Powys is dedicated.

MYMBYR (m)

A stream near Capel Curig in Gwynedd; the book *I Bought a Mountain* (1940) by Thomas Firbank is set in the district.

MYNORYDD (m)

MYNYDDOG (m)

from *mynydd*, a mountain.
Mynyddog Mwynfawr was leader of the Britons at the battle of Catraeth.

MYRDDIN (m) MERDDYN (m)

Myrddin Emrys was a magician in the court of king Arthur; he is known in English as Merlin (sometimes spelt Merlyn).

MYRIEL (f)

see Meriel.

N

NAMORA (f)

NAN (f) NANNO (f) NANW (f)

pet forms of Ann.

NANLYS (f)

NANNO (f)

see Nan.

NANNON (f)

a diminutive form of Rhiannon.

NANS (f) NANSI (f)

Nancy.

NANSI (f)

see Nans.

NANT (f)

a stream

NANTLAIS (m)

nant, a stream + *clais*, a ditch or *llais*, a voice.
Nantlais Williams (1874–1959) was a well-known hymn-writer.

NANW (f)

see Nan.

NANWEN (f)

NEDA (f)

NEDDIG (m)

A warrior mentioned in *Y Gododdin*.

NEDW (m)

a pet form of Ned (Edward).

NEFYDD (mf)

The daughter of Brychan Brycheiniog in the 5th century. William Roberts (1813–72), printer and writer, was known by his bardic name, Nefydd.

NEFYL (m)

Neville.

NEFYN (mf)

One of the daughters of Brychan Brycheiniog. The village of Nefyn is in Gwynedd.

NEIFION (m)

The Welsh name for Neptune.

NEIRIN (m)

see Aneirin.

NEIRTHIAD (m)

from *nerth*, strength.
A warrior praised for his valour in *Y Gododdin*.

NENNOG (m)

NERYS (f)

the feminine form of *nêr*, a lord.
Nerys Hughes is a well-known actress.

NEST (f) NESTA (f)

diminutive forms of Agnes.
Nest, the daughter of Rhys ap Tewdwr, the last king of south-west Wales, was renowned for her beauty and was known as 'the Helen of Wales' on account of her abduction by Owain ap Cadwgan in 1109; she had many lovers, including King Henry I, and was reputed to have borne at least seventeen children.

NESTA (f)

see Nest.

NIA (f)

An Irish name popularized in Wales by the poet T. Gwynn Jones (1871–1949). In Irish legend, Nia went with Osian to Tir na n-Og, the land of youth. Nia Roberts is a popular broadcaster.

NICLAS (m)

from Greek, victory.
Nicholas.
The Marxist poet Thomas Evan Nicholas (1878–1971) was popularly known as Niclas y Glais (because he had lived at Glais in the Swansea valley).

NIDIAN (m)

An early saint.

NINIAN (m)

Ninian Park was the home of Cardiff City Football Club until 2009.

NISIEN (m)

The half-brother of Efnisien in the Mabinogion.

NOELWYN (m) NOELYN (m)

from Noel.

NOELYN (m)

see Noelwyn.

NON (f) NONN (f) NONA (f) NONNA (f)

A saint in the 5th/6th century; she was the mother of Dewi (St. David) and her feast-day is 2 March.

NONA (f)

see Non.

NONN (f)

see Non.

NONNA (f)

see Non.

NOW (m)

Pet form of Owain.

NUDD (m)

A magician and brother of the king of the Underworld.

NWTHON (m)

The father of Heinif, a warrior praised in *Y Gododdin*.

NYFAIN (f)

O

ODWYN (m)

OEREINWEN (f)

OGWEN (m) OGWYN (f)

A river and valley in Gwynedd; John Ogwen is a distinguished actor. Rhodri Ogwen is a popular television presenter.

OGWYN (m)

see Ogwen.

OLAF (m)

last.

OLEULI (m)

OLFA (f)

OLGAN (m)

OLWEN (f) OLWENNA (f)

ôl, trace + *gwen*, white.
The daughter of Ysbaddaden Bencawr in the Mabinogion; her father sets Culhwch a number of near-impossible tasks before he can win her hand in marriage. Of Olwen it is said that wherever she trod, white trefoils sprang up, but this may be an onomastic explanation of her name.

OLWENNA (f)

see Olwen.

ONFAEL (m)

A village in Powys.

ONFEL (m)

ONLLWYN (m)

onn, an ash + *llwyn*, a grove.
A village in the Dulais valley in Powys David Onllwyn Brace played rugby union for Wales between 1956 and 1961.

ONNEN (m)

ONWEN (m)

ORCHWY

A tributary of the Rhondda, also called the Orci, on which Treorci stands.

ORIEL (m)

a gallery.
Oriel Jones gave his name to a well-known firm based in Llanybydder.

ORIG (m)

see Orwig.

ORLLWYN (m)

O

ORONWEN (f)

ORTHIN (m)

ORWIG (m) ORIG (m)

The former slate-mining village of Dinorwig is in Gwynedd. Orig Williams is a renowned wrestler.

OSFAEL (m)

One of the sons of Cunedda.

OSIAN (m)

A poet in Irish legend; Osian Ellis is a well-known Welsh harpist.

OSWALLT (m)

Oswald (Old English).
The Welsh name for Oswestry is Croesoswallt (Oswald's Cross).

OSWYN (m)

OWAIN (m) OWEN (m) OWENA (f)

well-born.
Owain Glyndwr (c. 1354–c. 1416), who led a revolt against English rule in Wales, is the national hero of the Welsh people.

OWEN (m)

see Owain.

OWENA (f)

see Owain.

P

PABO (m)

An early saint to whom the church at Llanbabo in Anglesey is dedicated.

PADARN (m)

from Latin, *paternus*, fatherly.
A 6th-century saint. The lake known as Llyn Padarn in Gwynedd and the village of Llanbadarn near Aberystwyth are named after him.

PADRIG (m)

from Latin, *patricus*, a nobleman.
Patrick.
The patron saint of Ireland (St. Patrick) was of Romano-Brythonic stock, having been born in western Britain. The church at Llanbadrig in Anglesey is dedicated to him.

PASGEN (m)

from *Pasg*, Easter.

PAWL (m)

from Latin, *paulus*, small.
Paul.

PEBLIG (m)

A saint commemorated at Llanbeblig in Gwynedd.

PEDR (m)

from Greek, *petros*, a stone or rock.
Peter.
Pedr Fardd was the bardic name of the hymn-writer Peter Jones (1775–1845).

PEDRAN (m) PETRAN (m)

diminutive forms of Pedr.

PEDROG (m)

A 6th-century saint, son of Glywys, king of Glamorgan, whose feast day is 4 June; Llanbedrog is a village in Gwynedd.

PELEG (m)

PENNANT (m)

pen, a head + *nant*, a stream.
Cwm Pennant is a celebrated valley in Gwynedd.

PENNAR (m)

A stream flowing into the Taff at Mountain Ash (Aberpennar) in Rhondda Cynon Taff. Pennar Davies (1911–96), who was born in the village, was a distinguished Welsh writer.

PENRI (m)

ap Henri, the son of Henry.
John Penry (1536–93) was a Puritan martyr.

PENWYN (m)

pen, head + *gwyn*, white.

PEREDUR (m)

Peredur the son of Efrog is the hero of a medieval tale; he is known in English as Percival.

PERIS (m) PERYS (m)

The lake known as Llyn Peris is near Llanberis in Gwynedd; Peris was not a saint, as is commonly assumed, but a man who lived sometime between the 11th and 12th centuries.

PERL (f)

Pearl.

PERNANT (m)

PERWEIR (f)

PERYF (m)

Peryf ap Cedifor Wyddel was foster-brother of the poet Hywel ab Owain Gwynedd in the 12th century.

PERYS (m)

see Peris.

PETRAN (m)

see Pedran.

PEULAN (m)

PHYLIP (m)

from Greek, a lover of horses Philip.

PLAENA (f)

PLENNYDD (m)

An early poet.

POWEL

ap Hywel, the son of Hywel.

POWYS (m)

An ancient kingdom and the modern county.

PRION (m)

PROSSER (m)

ap Rhosier, the son of Rhosier.
E. Prosser Rhys (1901–45) was a well-known Welsh poet.

PRYDAIN (m) PRYDYN (m)

Britain.

PRYDDERCH (m)

ap Rhydderch, the son of Rhydderch.

PRYDERI (m)

The son of Pwyll and Rhiannon in the Mabinogion.

PRYDWEN (mf) PRYDWYN (m)

pryd, complexion + *gwen* and *gwyn*, white The name of Arthur's ship and, according to Geoffrey of Monmouth, his shield.

PRYDWYN (m)

see Prydwen.

PRYDYN (m)

see Prydain.

PRYS (m)

ap Rhys, the son of Rhys.
Prys Morgan is a distinguished historian.

P

PRYSOR (m) PRYSORWEN (f)

A stream in Meirionnydd, celebrated in a poem by Hedd Wyn (Ellis Humphrey Evans, 1887–1917).

PRYSORWEN (m)

see Prysor.

PWYLL (m)

discretion, steadfastness.
The lord of Dyfed and husband of Rhiannon in the Mabinogion.

PYLL (m)

A warrior who, at the battle of Catraeth, 'paid for his mead-feast with his life'.

PYRS (m)

A name derived either from Pedr or Peris Siôn Pyrs was a leading figure in the Welsh television industry.

Q

There is no Q in the Welsh language.

R

RAHAWD (m)

Rahawd the son of Morgant is named in the Triads as one of 'the Three Frivolous Bards of the Isle of Britain'.

RAINILLT (f)

The daughter of Gruffudd ap Cynan.

REBECA (f) BECA (f)

a biblical name.
Rebekah, Rebecca.
The Rebecca Riots took place in southwest Wales in the mid-19th century; men dressed as women attacked toll-gates, taking their name from the Book of Genesis (24:60): 'And they blessed Rebekah and said unto her... Let thy seed possess the gate of those which hate them'.

RENALLT (m)

RHAGFEL (m)

RHAGFYRUN (m)

Rhagfyr, December.

RHAGNELL (f)

The mother of Gruffudd ap Cynan in the 11th century.

RHAIN (m)

a lance or spear.
Rhain ap Cadwgan was king of Dyfed in the 9th century.

RHEDINOG (m)

RHEDYN (f)

a fern.

RHEDYNOG (m)

RHEGED (m)

An old British territory in what is today the north of England.

RHEINALLT (m)

Hywel ap Rheinallt was a poet in the 15th century.

RHEITHFYW (m)

A warrior described in *Y Gododdin* as 'a pillar of battle'.

RHEON (m)

RHEUDROES (f)

RHIAIN (f) RHIAN (f) RIAN (f) RHIANNA (f)

a maiden.

RHIAINWEN (f)

see Rhianwen.

RHIAN (f)

see Rhiain.

RHIANEDD (f) RHIANYDD (f)

RHUANEDD (f)

from Rhian or Rhiain.

RHIANGAR (f) RHIENGAR (f)

rhian, a maiden + *câr*, love.

RHIANNA (f)

see Rhiain.

RHIANNON (f)

The wife of Pwyll and mother of Pryderi in the Mabinogion; the name may have been derived from that of the Celtic goddess Rigantona.

RHIANWEN (f) RHIAINWEN (f)

rhian, a maiden + *gwen*, white.

RHIANYDD (f)

see Rhianedd.

RHICERT (m)

Richard.

RHIDDID (m)

RHIDIAN (m)

see Rhydian.

RHIELL (mf)

RHYDION (m)

see Rhydian.

RHIENGAR (f)

a variant form of Rhiangar.

RHINA (f)

RHINEDD (f)

RHINOGWEN (f)

RHION (m)

RHIRID (m) RHIRYD (m)

rhi, a ruler + *rhidd*, to repel. Rhirid Flaidd was lord of Powys in the 12th century.

RHIRYD (m)

see Rhirid.

RHISIAN (f) RHYSIAN (f)

RHISIART (m)

Richard.

RHISIERDYN (m)

Richard.

RHIWALLON (m)

rhi, a ruler + *gwallon*, a ruler. Rhiwallon was the father of the Physicians of Myddfai in medieval times.

RHOBAT (m)

see Robat.

R

RHOBET (m)

see Robat.

RHODD (mf)

a gift.

RHODRI (m)

rhod, a circle + *rhi*, a ruler.
Rhodri Fawr was king of Gwynedd, Powys and Deheubarth in the 9th century. Rhodri Morgan was elected as First Minister for the National Assembly in February 2000.

RHONA (f)

a diminutive form of Rhonwen.

RHONABWY (m)

The hero of one of the Arthurian tales dating from about the mid-12th century; Rhonabwy spends the night at the hall of Heilyn Coch in Powys and has a splendid dream in which he is transported to Arthur's encampment on an island in the river Severn.

RHONDA (f)

This name is popularly thought to be a variant of Rhondda, the famous coal-valley in south Wales, and enjoyed a brief vogue because it was borne by the filmstar Rhonda Fleming.

RHONDDA (mf)

see Rhonda.

RHONWEN (f)

The Welsh form of Rowena (see under Alys), daughter of Hengist, with whom Vortigern fell in love, according to Geoffrey of Monmouth.

RHOSAN (f)

a river in Powys.

RHOSIER (m)

Roger.

RHOSLYN (mf) ROSLYN (mf)

rhos, a rose or moor + *glyn*, a valley.

RHOSWEN (f)

rhos, a rose or moor + *gwen*, fair.

RHOSWY (f)

RHOSYDD (mf)

RHUANEDD (f)

see Rhianedd.

RHUDDIAN (f)

RHUFAWN (m)

see Rhufon.

RHUFON (m) RHUFAWN (m)

One of the sons of Cunedda who gave his name to Rhufoniog, a district in north-east Wales.

RHUN (m) RHUNEDD (f)

grand.
A character in the tale of Taliesin.

RHUNEDD (f)

see Rhun.

RHUNLI (m)

RHUNOGWEN (f)

RHYDDAN (m)

A stream in Carmarthenshire.

RHYDDERCH (m)

rhi, a ruler + *derch*, exalted.
Rhydderch Hael was an ally of Urien Rheged in the 6th century. The name is anglicized as Ruddock.

RHYDDID (m)

freedom.

RHYDFEN (m)

RHYDIAN (m) RHYDION (m) RHIDIAN (m)

An early saint commemorated at Llanrhidian in Gower.

RHYDWEN (m) RHYDWENFRO (m) RHYDWYN (m)

rhyd, a ford + *gwen*, white.
Rhydwen Williams (1916–97) was a distinguished poet and novelist; his full name was Rhydwenfro.

RHYDWENFRO (m)

see Rhydwen.

RHYDWYN (m)

see Rhydwen.

RHYGYFARCH (m)

One of the four sons of Sulien, he was a monk who wrote a Life of St. David.

RHYS (m)

ardour.
Rhys ap Gruffudd (The Lord Rhys) was lord of south-west Wales in the 14th century; the name is anglicized to Rees, Rice and Reece. Rhys Ifans is a well-known actor.

RHYSTUD

A 6th-century saint who is commemorated at Llanrhystud in Ceredigion.

RHYSYN (m)

a pet form of Rhys.

RIAN (f)

see Rhian.

ROBART (m)

see Robat.

ROBAT (m) ROBART (m) RHOBAT (m) ROBET (m) RHOBET (m)

Robert.

ROBET (m)

see Robat.

ROBYN (m) ROBYNA (f)

diminutive forms of Robat.

ROBYNA (f)

see Robyn.

R

RODRIC (m)

another form of Rhydderch.
The anglicized form of this name is
Roderick.

ROLANT (m)

Roland.

RONW (m)

see Goronwy.

RONWEN (f)

see Rhonwen.

ROSENTYL (f)

ROSLYN (mf)

see Roslyn.

RUDDRHOS (f)

S

SADWRN (m) SADYRNIN (m)

Saturday, Saturn.
An early saint commemorated at Llansadwrn in Carmarthenshire.

SADYRNIN (m)

see Sadwrn.

SAERAN (f) SARAN (f) SERAN (f)

SAERON (m)

A saint to whom the church at Llanynys in Denbighshire is dedicated; there is a village of the same name in Powys.

SAMLET (m)

A saint commemorated at Llansamlet, near Swansea.

SANANT (f)

The mother of Elisedd, king of Powys, and wife of Maelgwn Gwynedd.

SANDDE (m)

A young man of Arthur's court who received no blow at the battle of Camlann because he was so beautiful.

SANNAN (m)

from Latin, *sanctus*, holy.
A stream in Denbighshire; the village of Llansannan is in the same county.

SARA (f)

from Hebrew, a princess.
Sarah.
Sara Edwards is a television newsreader and broadcaster.

SARAN (f)

see Saeron.

SAWEL (m) SAWYL (m)

Samuel.
A 6th-century saint who is commemorated at Llansawel in Carmarthenshire; Llansawel is also the Welsh name of Briton Ferry.

SAWYL (m)

see Sawel.

SEFIN (m) SEFION (m)

A stream in Carmarthenshire.

SEFION (m)

see Sefin.

SEFNYN (m)

A poet from Anglesey in the 14th century.

SEIMON (m)

Simon.

SEIRIAL (mf)

see Seiriol.

SEIRIAN (m)

sparkling.

SEIRIOL (m) SEIRIAL (f)

The founder of Penmon church in Anglesey in the 6th century whose feast-day is 1 February.

SEISYLL (m) SEISYLLT (m) SITSYLL (m)

from Latin, Sextilius.
Seisyllt ap Clydog was lord of Gwynedd in the 10th century; this name was angli-cized to Cecil.

SEISYLLT (m)

see Seisyll.

SEITHENNYN (m) SEITHNYN (m)

The drunken watchman who allowed the sea to invade Cantre'r Gwaelod in what is today Cardigan Bay.

SEITHNYN (m)

see Seithennyn.

SELINDA (f)

SELWYN (m)

sêl, ardour + *gwyn*, white or blessèd.

SELYF (m)

from Hebrew, a small man of peace.
Solomon.
Selyf ap Cynan led the Welsh in the battle of Chester in 613.

SELYN (m)

SENYLLT (m)

A warrior mentioned in *Y Gododdin*.

SERAN (f)

see Saeran.

SEREN (mf)

a star.

SERIAN (f)

SGEIRWYN (m)

SHAN (f) SHÂN (f)

see Siân.

SHON (m) SHÔN (m)

see Siôn.

SIABOD (m)

Moel Siabod is a mountain in Gwynedd.

SIAMAS (m)
see Siams.

SIAMS (m) SIAMAS (m)

James.

SIÂN (f) SHAN (f) SHANI (f)

Jane.
Siân Phillips is a distinguished actress and Siân Lloyd presents the weather-forecast on ITV.

SIANCO (m)

a pet form of Siencyn.

SIANI (f)

a diminutive form of Siân.

SIARL (m) SIARLYS (m)

Charles.

SIARLYS (m)

see Siarl.

SIDAN (f)

silk.

SIEFFRE (m)

Geoffrey, Jeffrey.
Sieffre o Fynwy (Geoffrey of Monmouth; c. 1090–1155) was a Latin writer and pseudo-historian of early Britain whose *Historia Regum Britanniae (History of the Kings of Britain)* claimed to trace the history of Britain from Brutus to Cadwaladr, the last British king, who lost the sovereignty of the island to the Saxons.

SIENCYN (m)

Jenkin.
The name Jenkin was brought into Wales by Flemish settlers in the 11th century.

SILFAN (m)

SILYN (m)

Cwm Silyn is a valley in Gwynedd. Robert Silyn Roberts (1871–1930) was a well-known poet.

SIMWNT (m)

Simon.
Simwnt Fychan was a poet from the Vale of Clwyd in the 16th century.

SIÔN (m) SHON (m) SHÔN (m)

John.
Siôn Cent was a poet in the early 15th century; Santa Claus is known in Welsh as Siôn Corn.

SIONED (f) SIONEN (f)

Janet.
a diminutive form of Siân or the feminine form of Siôn.

SIONEN (f)

see Sioned.

SIONI (m) SIONYN (m)

diminutive forms of Siôn.

SIONYN (m)

see Sioni.

SIOR (m)

George.

SIRIOL (f)

cheerful.

S

SITSYLL (m)

see Seisyll.

SIWAN (f)

Joan.
The daughter of King John of England, who was married to Llywelyn Fawr in the 13th century, was known in Welsh as Siwan.

SIWSAN (f)

Susan.

SOFLAN (m)

STEFFAN (m) STYFIN (m) STYFFAN (m) YSTYFFAN (m) YSTYFYN (m)

from Greek, a crown.
Stephen, Steven.
Stephen was the first Christian martyr; his feast-day is 26 December. But there was also a native British saint of this name. Llansteffan is in Carmarthenshire and Westminster is known in Welsh as San Steffan.

STYFFAN (m)

see Steffan.

STYFIN (m)

see Steffan.

SULCWYN (m)

SULGEN (m)

A river in Carmarthenshire.

SULIAN (f)

see Sulien.

SULIEN (m) SULIAN (m)

sul, the sun + *geni*, to be born.
The Celtic sun-god and an early saint who was bishop of St. David's in the 11th century.

SULWEN (f) SULWYN (m)

sul, the sun + *gwen* or *gwyn*, white.
Sulwyn Thomas is a well-known broadcaster.

SURWEN (f)

charming, magical.

SYCHARTH (m)

The home, near the Shropshire border, of Owain Glyndwr, the national hero of Wales.

SYLWEN (f)

T

TAFF (m) TAFFY (mf)

a diminutive form of Dafydd or perhaps from the river Taff (Tâf) on which the towns of Merthyr Tydfil and Pontypridd and the city of Cardiff stand.

Often used by the English as a nickname, not always insultingly, for any Welshman (cf. Jock for a Scotsman, Paddy for an Irishman); in the USA Taffy is a feminine name.

TAFFY (m)

see Taff.

TAFLOYW (m)

One of the warriors who fell at the battle of Catraeth.

TAFWYS (mf)

The Welsh name for the river Thames.

TAFYDD (m)

from Tâf (Taff), the rivers in south and south-west Wales.

TALDWYN (m)

TALFAN (m)

tal, tall + *ban*, a beacon.
Aneirin Talfan Davies (1909–80) was a well-known writer and broadcaster.

TALFRYN (m)

tal, tall + *bryn*, a hill.

TALFOR (m)

TALHAIARN (m)

tal, tall or *tâl*, a brow + *haearn*, iron.
The bardic name of John Jones (1810–70), who was born in the village of Llanfair Talhaearn in Denbighshire.

TALIEN (f)

TALIESIN (m)

tâl, a brow + *iesin*, radiant.
A poet who flourished in northern Britain in the 6th century; also the son of the goddess Ceridwen. The architect Frank Lloyd Wright (1867–1959), who was of Welsh descent, called one of his homes Taliesin.

TALOG (m)

A village in Gwynedd.

TALWYN (m)

TANAD (m) TANAT (m)

A valley in Powys.

TANAT (m)

see Tanad.

TANGLWST (f)

see Tangwystl.

TANGNO (m)

from *tangnefedd*, peace.
Collwyn ap Tangno is reputed to have founded one of the fifteen royal tribes of Wales.

T

TANGWEN (f) TANGWYN (m)

from *tangnefedd*, peace + *gwen* or *gwyn*, white or blessèd.

TANGWYN (m)

see Tangwen.

TANGWYSTL (f) TANGLWST (f)

tangnefedd, peace + *gwystl*, a hostage or pledge.
A daughter of Brychan Brycheiniog and the wife of Cyngen ap Cadell.

TANNO (f)

a diminutive form of Tangwystl.

TANWEN (f)

tân, fire + *gwen*, white.

TARAN (m)

thunder.

TARYN (f)

TATHAL (m)

A character in the tale of Culhwch and Olwen; the Irish form of Tudwal.

TATHAN (m)

A 5th-century saint and the patron saint of Chepstow; his feast-day is 26 December and he is commemorated at St. Athan (Sain Tathan) in the Vale of Glamorgan.

TAWE (m)

The name of the river on which Swansea (Abertawe) stands.

TECWYN (m)

teg, fair + *gwyn* or *gwen*, white.
Tecwyn, an early saint, is commemorated at Llandecwyn in Meirionydd.

TEFYDD (m)

TEGAI (mf)

An early saint commemorated at Llandygái in Gwynedd.

TEGAN (f) TEGAU (f)

teg, fair + diminutive *an*.
An early saint and a stream in Ceredigion.
The modern meaning of *tegan* is toy.

TEGAU (f)

see Tegan.

TEGEIRIAN (mf)

teg, fair + *eirian*, beautiful or orchid.

TEGERYN (m)

TEGFAN (m)

teg, fair + *ban*, summit or *man*, place.

TEGFEDD (f)

A sister of Tydecho, a 6th-century saint. Llandegfedd is in Monmouthshire.

TEGFRYN (m)

teg, fair + *bryn*, a hill.

TEGID (m) TEGIDWEN (f)

from Latin, Tacitus.
Llyn Tegid near Bala is named after Tegid
Foel who, in the tale of Taliesin, was re-
puted to live in the lake.

TEGIDWEN (f)

see Tegid.

TEGLA (m)

A saint commemorated at Llandegla in
Denbighshire. E. Tegla Davies (1880–
1967), who was born in the village, was a
popular writer and broadcaster.

TEGRYN (m)

A saint commemorated at Llanegryn in
Gwynedd.

TEGWAL (m)

see Tegwel.

TEGWEDD (f)

teg, fair + *gwedd*, appearance.

TEGWEL (m) TEGWAL (m)

a form of Degwel.

TEGWEN (f)

see Tegwyn.

TEGWYN (m) TEGWEN (f)

teg, fair + *gwyn* or *gwen*, white.

TEGWYTH (f)

TEGYR (f)

TEIDDWEN (f)

a form of Eiddwen.

TEIFI (m) TEIFINA (f) TEIFWEN (f)

A river in Ceredigion on which the town
of Cardigan (Aberteifi) stands. Hywel
Teifi Edwards is a renowned historian
and orator.

TEIFINA (f)

see Teifi.

TEIFION (m)

a variant of Eifion.

TEIFRYN

Teifi + *bryn*, a hill.

TEILO (m)

A 6th-century saint who preached in south
Wales and Brittany; he is commemorated
at Llandeilo in Carmarthenshire.

TEITHFYW (m)

A warrior from Anglesey who is celebrated in *Y Gododdin*.

TELAID (f)

beautiful.

T

TELERCH (m)

A name associated with Rumney (Tredelerch) near Cardiff.

TELERI (f)

A form of Eleri.
The name of rivers in west and south-east Wales; Abertyleri stands where the stream Tyleri joins the Ebwy Fach river.

TELIDWEN (f)

TELOR (m) DELOR (m)

from *telori*, to sing.

TEON (m)

TERFEL (m)

a form of Derfel.
Bryn Terfel is a well-known opera singer.

TERRIG (m)

TERWIN (m)

see Terwyn.

TERWYN (m) TERWIN (m)

têr, bright + *gwyn*, white.

TESNI (f)

warmth.

TEWDRID (m)

The grandfather of Brychan Brycheiniog.

TEWDWR (m)

see Tudur.

TEYRNON (m)

The lord of Gwent Iscoed in the Mabinogion; the 'great king' in Celtic religion.

TIRION (f)

gentle, happy.

TOMI (m)

a diminutive form of Tomos.

TOMOS (m)

from Aramaic, a twin.
Thomas.
One of the twelve apostles of Jesus Christ.

TONWEN (f)

ton, wave + *gwen*, white.

TOSTIG (m)

TOWY (m)

see Tywi.

TOWYN (m)

see Tywyn.

TRAHAEARN (m)

tra, great + *haearn*, iron.
Trahaearn Brydydd Mawr was a poet in the 14th century.

TREBOR (m)

the name Robert spelt in reverse.
Trebor Mai (I am Robert) was the bardic name of Robert Williams (1830–77). Trebor Edwards is a popular singer.

TREFINA (f)

TREFLYN (m)

TREFOR (m)

tref, a home or town + *mor*, great or sea
This name is anglicized as Trevor.

TREGELLYS (m)

Tregelles.

TRISTAN (m)

see Trystan.

TRYDDID (m)

TRYDWYN (m)

TRYFAN (m) TRYFANA (f)

A mountain in Gwynedd.

TRYFANWY (m)

TRYGARN (m)

TRYSTAN (m) TRISTAN (m) DRYSTAN (m)

The hero of the tale of Trystan and Esyllt. Trystan, the nephew of Marc of Cornwall, is sent to Ireland to fetch Esyllt so that she can be married to the king, but on the return journey they inadvertently drink the love-potion given to them by Brengain. They fall in love and flee to the forest of Broceliande in Brittany.

TUDFOR (m)

tud, land + *mor*, great or sea.

TUDFUL (f) TUDFYL (f) TYDFIL (f) TYDFILIN (m) ARDUDFYL (f)

A saint, the daughter of Brychan Brycheiniog; according to tradition, she was martyred (or buried) near where Merthyr Tydfil stands today.

TUDFWLCH (m)

One of the warriors who fell at the battle of Catraeth.

TUDFYL (f)

see Tudful.

TUDNO (m)

A saint commemorated in the place-name Llandudno on the coast of north Wales.

TUDRI (m)

tud, land or tribe + *rhi*, a ruler.

TUDRIG (m)

a form of Tudur.

T

TUDUR (m) TEWDWR (m)

Henry Tudor, who was of Welsh descent, is known in Welsh as Harri Tudur. Tudur Aled was a poet in the 15th/16th century. The name is anglicized as Tudor.

TUDWAL (m)

tud, a country or tribe + *gwal*, a ruler.

TWELI (m)

The river Tyweli is in Carmarthenshire. Tweli Griffiths is a well-known broadcaster.

TWM (m)

a diminutive form of Tomos.
Twm o'r Nant (Edward Williams, 1738–1810) was a writer of interludes. Twm Morys is a contemporary poet and musician.

TWYNOG (m)

TYBIE (f)

A saint and daughter of Brychan Brycheiniog who is commemorated at Llandybie in Carmarthenshire.

TYBION (m)

TYDECHO (m)

A 6th-century saint.

TYDFIL (m)

see Tudful.

TYDFILYN (m)

see Tudful.

TYDFOR (m)

TYDWEN (f)

TYFRIOG (m)

a diminutive form of Briafael.

TYFRION (m)

TYFYRIOG (m)

see Briog.

TYLERI (f)

see Teleri.

TYNGYR (m)

A warrior whose death is celebrated in *Y Gododdin*.

TYNORO (m)

TYSILIO (m)

A 7th-century saint and son of Brochfael who is commemorated at Llantysilio in Anglesey.

TYSUL (m)

a familiar form of Sulien.
A saint of this name is commemorated at Llandysul in Ceredigion.

TYWI (m) TOWY (m)

A river in Carmarthenshire.

TYWYN (m) TOWYN (m)

A town in Gwynedd.
The Rev. J. Towyn Jones (1858–1925)

was Liberal M.P. for Carmarthen East 1912–18 and Llanelli 1918–22.

TYWYNNOG (m)

a pet form of Gwyn.

U

UNDEG (f)

un, one + *deg*, fair.

UNGOED (m)

un, one + *coed*, trees.
A.L. Ungoed-Thomas was Labour MP for Llandaff and Barry (1945–50).

URFAI (m)

A warrior mentioned in *Y Gododdin*.

URIEL (m)

URIEN (m)

from Brythonic, *Urbigenos*, twin-born Urien Rheged was lord of the Britons in the 6th century. Urien William (1930–2006) was a distinguished author and dramatist.

V

There is no V in the modern Welsh alphabet.

W

WATCYN (m)
a form of Gwatcyn.

WEDROS (m)

The village of Caerwedros is in Ceredigion.

WENA (f) WENNA (f)

diminutive forms of Awena and Morwena.

WENHAF (f)

WENNA (f)

see Wenna.

WENORA (f)

WERNOS (m)

WIL (m)

a diminutive form of Gwilym and William Wil Ifan (William Evans, 1888–1968) was a popular poet.

WINONA (f)

Winona Ryder is a popular American actress.

WILIAM (m)

William.

WMFFRE (m)

Humphrey.

WYN (m) WYNN (m)

gwyn, white or blessèd.
a variant of Gwyn.
Ieuan Wyn Jones is a Plaid Cymru member of the National Assembly.

WYNALLT (m)

WYNDRAETH (m)

see Gwendraeth.

WYNN (m)

see Wyn.

WYNONA (f)

WYRE (m)

A river in Ceredigion.
Wyre Davies is a news broadcaster.

Y

YDFRAN (m)

YDWENNA (f)

YNYR (m) **YNYRA** (f) **INYR** (m)
INIR (m)

from Latin, *honorius*, reputation
Emyr is a variant form.

YNYRA (f)

see Ynyr.

YSBADDADEN (m)

The king of the giants and father of
Olwen in the Mabinogion.

YSBWYS (m)

YSFAEL (m)

One of the sons of Cunedda.

YSGIR (m)

Aberysgir is a village in Powys.

YSGYRRAN (m)

A warrior mentioned in *Y Gododdin*.

YSTWYTH (m)

A river in Ceredigion from which
Aberystwyth takes its name.

YSTYFFAN (m)

see Steffan.

YSTYFYN (m)

see Steffan.

YWAIN (m)

a form of Owain.

Z

There is no Z in the Welsh alphabet.

For further reading

T. D. Breverton, *The Book of Welsh Saints* (Glyndwr Publishing 2000).

Gwyn Jones & Thomas Jones (trans.), *The Mabinogion* (Dent, 1949, with many subsequent edns.).

Thomas Parry, trans., H. Idris Bell, *A History of Welsh Literature* (Oxford University Press, 1955).

Gwyn Jones, *Welsh Legends and Folktales* (Oxford University Press, 1955).

Elwyn Davies, *A Gazetteer of Welsh Place-names* (University of Wales Press, 1958).

H. Meurig Evans & W.O. Thomas, *Y Geiriadur Mawr: The Complete Welsh-English, English-Welsh Dictionary* (Christopher Davies and Gwasg Gomer, 1958, with many subsequent edns.).

J.E. Lloyd & R.T. Jenkins (eds.), *The Dictionary of Welsh Biography down to 1940* (Blackwell for the Hon. Soc. of Cymmrodorion, 1959) with supplements to 1950 and 1970.

Joseph P. Clancy (trans.), *Medieval Welsh Lyrics* (Macmillan, 1965).

Joseph P. Clancy (trans.), *The Earliest Welsh Poetry* (Macmillan, 1970).

David Hugh Farmer, *The Oxford Dictionary of Saints* (Oxford University Press, 1978).

T.J. Morgan & Prys Morgan, *Welsh Surnames* (University of Wales Press, 1985).

A.O.H. Jarman, *Y Gododdin* (Gomer, 1988).

Tony Conran, *Welsh Verse* (Seren, 1992).

Meic Stephens (ed.), *The Oxford Illustrated Literary Guide to Great Britain and Ireland* (Oxford University Press; 2nd edn., 1992).

Janet Davies, *The Welsh Language* (University of Wales Press, 1993).

John Davies, *A History of Wales* (Allen Lane: The Penguin Press, 1993).

Dafydd Johnston, *The Literature of Wales: A Pocket Guide* (University of Wales Press, 1994).

Bruce Griffiths & Dafydd Glyn Jones, *The Welsh Academy English-Welsh Dictionary* (University of Wales Press, 1995).

A.O.H. Jarman & G.R. Hughes (eds.), revised by Dafydd Johnston, *A Guide to Welsh Literature c.1282–1550* (University of Wales Press, 1997).

R. Geraint Gruffydd (ed.), *A Guide to Welsh Literature c. 1530–1700* (University of Wales Press, 1997).

Dafydd Johnston (ed.), *A Guide to Welsh Literature c. 1900–1996* (University of Wales Press, 1998).

James MacKillop, *Dictionary of Celtic Mythology* (Oxford University Press, 1998).

Hywel Wyn Owen, *The Place-Names of Wales* (University of Wales Press & *The Western Mail*, 1998).

Meic Stephens (ed.), *The New Companion to the Literature of Wales* (University of Wales Press, 1998).

P. Hanks, F. Hodges, A.D. Mills, A. Room, *The Oxford Names Companion* (Oxford University Press, 1998).

Meic Stephens, *The Literary Pilgrimin Wales* (Carreg Gwalch, 2001).